Table of Contents

Legal Disclaimer

FORWARD

Thanks for purchasing "**Creating The Identity of Your New Business**" I have authored this book for those people who have questions as to what they should do with their start-up business in terms of protection and the creation of your identity.

Most people with start-ups assume correctly that they have to protect their brand name with a trademark. They are correct, but simultaneously, there are a number of other things to consider and many can be done for free.

We will examine a number of areas that should be considered and you will be able to make decisions and take action right away while you are reading this book. When it comes to business knowledge is a form of currency that can be put to use in order to make money.

One thing I do enjoy doing with the Low Cost Empire Series is making sure that I cover a lot of ground in a way that is easy to understand and then easy to capitalize on.

This book, just as the other books in this series help the entrepreneur to wear many hats effectively.

The book will unfold comfortably for you and you will feel like you are attending a seminar. There is a lot of strategy in this book so do read it thoroughly.

Enjoy the book and I will see you at the conclusion.

Creating The Identity of Your New Business

Establishing An Identity
Checking Your Proposed Name for Availability:

Let's Start Out With Trademark Availability:

I am not going to give you a course on filing a trademark in this particular book because we have so much to cover of value that will help you immensely. I have already authored a thorough book on filing your trademark from beginning to end. You can purchase it on **lowcostempire.com**. What I will do, in the interest of a smooth flow, is to give you a **very good and thorough overview** of why you first need to check into the trademark question. If we do not know what is going on in terms of the availability of the proposed trademark name, then there is no point doing anything else since you are just playing with fire. So, let us go over why we need to know what is going on in terms of trademark availability.

Whatever area you are working in, you will need to establish an identity. You will want to have a firmly established **trade name** for your invention, service, company etc. You don't want to go to a venture capitalist or any company or bank seeking money if you don't even know what you are going to name your project or venture. We have to be sure that whatever we choose to name our entity; we want to know that it is a name that is unique and not already protected by another individual or company. Below is a thorough **mini-lesson** on dealing with your

trademark search. Keep in mind that if you need to do a trademark and you have the funds then let an attorney do it. If you don't have the funds do not let this stop you from moving forward. My book **"Getting Down To Business – Filing Your First Trademark"**, will hand hold and baby step you through the whole process and you have me to contact as always if you should need to. I am one of the few authors that will field questions and attempt to help.

Mini Lesson On Trademarks:

Do not underestimate the above question. The reason that you care about the trademark is for the following reasons. If the name you had hoped to use is **already trademarked**, meaning that someone else has the **sole right** to use that name in all 50 states, you would then want to seriously consider coming up with another name. The reason for going back to the drawing board is that the person or company already using that name **in that same line of business** (same international classification) as yours can legally sue you and effectively **prohibit you** from using the name anyway, so please don't waste your time. Simply go back to the "drawing board" and come up with another name. Chances are that the next one you come up with might be **unique** and you won't have to worry about any trademark issues. In order to search the trademark data base to see if your proposed business name/trade name is already secured and registered **by someone else**, you would go to http://www.uspto.gov and look for the "**Trademarks**" section as shown below:

Under **Trademarks** TRADEMARKS go to "Search and then Use the "**New User Search**".

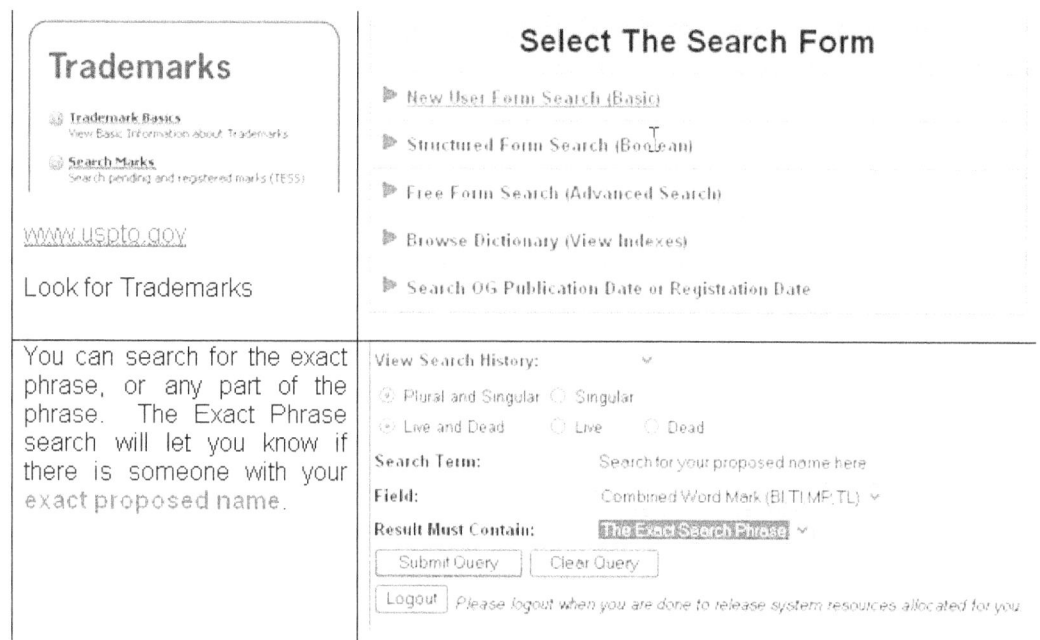

Now, if there is a match, check to see whether it is a "**live**" or "**dead**" filing. A dead filing simply means that the former owner did not file the appropriate documents and/or pay the required fees to maintain the trademark for whatever reason, and decided to **abandon** the trademark.

If it is a **dead filing**, you do not have to worry. The dead filings are marks that have been **abandoned** due to lapse of fees or the owner simply lost interest. If the search comes up with "**no hits**" then you can be sure to a high degree of certainty that the name is available for trademark protection. You can file on-line for a trademark by following the instructions carefully

If your initial search comes up clean (meaning no matches) then do the following. Search for any words of your proposed mark and see what comes up. Search for different uses or spellings of common words such as **Car Fax** or **Kar Fax** or **Kids World** or **Kidz world (Example of Pseudo marks)**. Be as thorough as you can as a non-legal professional. If your name is for example **The World Group**, search it out for **World Group, Our World Group, World Group Leaders etc.** Don't just get excited because there was not an initial direct hit.

Take your time and be thorough. If another filing is in the system, whether it be Pending **(TM)** or Registered ® or yet to be examined but nevertheless in the system before you, the Trademark Examiner can determine that your particular filing is **a bit too close** to the already existing filing and can **reject** your application and you then lose **$325.00** hard earned dollars. **Do the work**. Be sure that your proposed mark is not already out there. Even if it is somewhat close you may have a problem, so don't do a lack luster job. **Search it out. Take a day or two to really search it out. Do the preliminary work before you file**. There is no need to lose your hard earned money. If it is already out there, then simply go back to the drawing board. I don't know about you, but I would rather have a **UNIQUE NAME** for a brand new venture that I came up with rather than a name that I **constantly** had to look **over my shoulder** because it is too similar to another name already in use.

The reason that I emphasize the trademark issue is because if you feel you have a great concept name, then moving for trademark protection is an extremely important step. If you think small you will simply stay small. Down the road, if you decide that you want to **Franchise** your business, you will need to "**own**" the rights to your name in all fifty states. The only way to achieve this is to be awarded a trademark. Another reason for needing a trademark is the **licensing** issue.

If, in the future, you find yourself wanting to enter into a licensing agreement, whereby an individual or company wants to **pay you for the right to use your name or logo** in some aspect of their business or to place your name or logo on some item like a cup, towel, clothing item, etc. then 1) you would only be in a position to enter into a licensing agreement if you did in fact **own the rights to the name and logo** under the classification of goods or 2) the classification of services that the prospective licensee is interested in. Otherwise, **THEY DON'T NEED YOU AND THEY WOULD SIMPLY USE THAT NAME OR LOGO WHENEVER THEY FELT LIKE IT WITH NO REPERCUSSIONS.** For licensing, you have to get the book **Licensing Your Invention by Richard Stim**. He totally introduces you to the world of licensing. Go to **Amazon or half.com**, look for a used copy and you will truly get an education that will allow you to talk the talk from his user friendly book.

It is important to point out that you can apply for a trademark on-line www.uspto.gov and the website has **step-by-step instructions** concerning the filing. In my book, I go over the entire process with you from beginning to end with a lot more insight. If you have a brand new business and have not sold any goods or services across state lines then you can file what is called an "**Intent to Use**" Trademark Application. If from the moment you started your business you have been selling interstate (**commerce between states**), whether it is goods or services, then you can file an "**In Use**" Trademark Application. Again, these applications have built-in instructions. The filing fee is **$325.00**.

If you have filed an **intent to use application**, once your mark is deemed by the trademark examiner to be worthy of being granted, you then have **5 chances** to **renew** your **Intent to Use status** (6 month increments) before you must convert the status to **IN USE** or else you must forfeit the mark. **When you do convert over to an In Use application that will cost you $100.00**. Note: If you initially file as In Use and submit your specimen from the start, you will have no reason to worry about the Intent to Use or the $100.00 dollar conversion fee. People who file the Intent to Use do so because they simply are not selling their item whether it be goods or services AS OF YET but they sure plan to.

Each extension of an Intent To Use (**and you can do this five times**) will cost you **one hundred fifty dollars per extension**. As soon as you start to make sales from customers residing in another state you can then **convert your "Intent-To-Use" status over to "In-Use"** by filing your **In-Use** application.

Whether you file as **In Use** or **Intent To Use**, at a certain point, you will receive notice that you are going into the **Official Gazette** to see if there is any opposition. The Gazette is the Trademark magazine so to speak where the public gets the chance to see if there are any marks that are being proposed that clash with an already existing mark. If there is NO OPPOSITION from another already existing Trademark holder or someone with a current Trademark Application, you will receive a Notice of Allowance **after the 30 day period. [If you do get opposition concerning your Gazette listing, you will be notified from the Trademark Office]**. Once you issue your **Statement of Use**, if you had not done so from the beginning, approximately 3 months later, **your trademark will issue** and you are then protected in all fifty states against anyone using your name without your permission. Keep in mind that you don't have to already have the trademark in order to seek money. It would be great if you at least filed an application and you are somewhere within the chronology of the application to show that you are aware of the need to protect the new brand.

Once you file for a trademark you should be using the "™" symbol after your proposed name wherever and whenever you use it. The "™" symbol alerts people that although a Trademark has not yet been granted, it lets them know that you are claiming the name as yours and you are **currently somewhere along the chronology of the Trademark Application process**. If you are in the "service business" then use the "**SM**" superscripted after the name of your company or product name on your business cards, and other items bearing the name. When you are issued the Trademark and it becomes Registered, and is no longer just a pending application, you will then place a "®" at the end of the mark and you will make sure that it is on everything and everywhere that your name appears. The "®" symbol lets people know that the mark is your property, **protected in all fifty states from infringement** or unauthorized use. For those of you that think you are protected by simply placing a "™" after your trade name well you are not. If you did not file an actual application then you placing a "™" after your trade name has no weight. If someone should look you up in the database and see you are not in there, they can file for your mark and undercut you and thus take your mark. Yes, depending on how long you have been using the mark in a certain region or location you can claim common law rights but someone else can take over the name with a trade mark and then you have cheated yourself, so take ownership of your trade name.

Look at the list below and make an attempt to determine what international classification that your trademark or service mark will fall under. Also, do consider purchasing my book Low Cost Empire – Getting Down to Business – Filing Your First Trademark.

International Schedule of Classes of Goods and Services

GOODS

1. chemicals used in industry, science and photography, as well as in agriculture, horticulture and forestry; unprocessed artificial resins; unprocessed plastics; manures; fire extinguishing compositions; tempering and soldering preparations; chemical substances for preserving foodstuffs; tanning substances; adhesives used in industry.
2. Paints, varnishes, lacquers; preservatives against rust and against deterioration of wood; colorants; mordants; raw natural resins; metals in foil and powder form for painters, decorators, printers and artists.
3. Bleaching preparations and other substances for laundry use; cleaning, polishing, scouring and abrasive preparations; soaps; perfumery, essential oils, cosmetics, hair lotions; dentifrices.
4. Industrial oils and greases; lubricants; dust absorbing, wetting and binding compositions; fuels (including motor spirit) and illuminants; candles, wicks.
5. Pharmaceutical, veterinary, and sanitary preparations; dietetic

substances adapted for medical use, food for babies; plasters, materials for dressings; material for stopping teeth, dental wax; disinfectants; preparations for destroying vermin; fungicides, herbicides.

6. Common metals and their alloys; metal building materials; transportable buildings of metal; materials of metal for railway tracks; non-electric cables and wires of common metal; ironmongery, small items of metal hardware; pipes and tubes of metal; safes; goods of common metal not included in other classes; ores.

7. Machines and machine tools; motors and engines (except for land vehicles); machine coupling and transmission components (except for land vehicles); agricultural implements other than hand-operated; incubators for eggs.

8. Hand tools and implements (hand-operated); cutlery; side arms; razors.

9. Scientific, nautical, surveying, electric, photographic, cinematographic, optical, weighing, measuring, signaling, checking (supervision), life-saving and teaching apparatus and instruments; apparatus for recording, transmission or reproduction of sound or images; magnetic data carriers, recording discs; automatic vending machines and mechanisms for coin operated apparatus; cash registers, calculating machines, data processing equipment and computers; fire extinguishing apparatus.

10. Surgical, medical, dental, and veterinary apparatus and instruments, artificial limbs, eyes, and teeth; orthopedic articles; suture materials.

11. Apparatus for lighting, heating, steam generating, cooking, refrigerating, drying, ventilating, water supply, and sanitary purposes.

12. Vehicles; apparatus for locomotion by land, air, or water.

13. Firearms; ammunition and projectiles; explosives; fireworks.

14. Precious metals and their alloys and goods in precious metals or coated therewith, not included in other classes; jewelry, precious stones; horological and chronometric instruments.

15. Musical instruments.

16. Paper, cardboard and goods made from these materials, not included in other classes; printed matter; bookbinding material; photographs; stationery; adhesives for stationery or household purposes; artists' materials; paint brushes; typewriters and office requisites (except furniture); instructional and teaching material (except apparatus); plastic materials for packaging (not included in other classes); playing cards; printers' type; printing blocks.

17. Rubber, gutta-percha, gum, asbestos, mica and goods made from these materials and not included in other classes; plastics in extruded form for use in manufacture; packing, stopping and insulating materials; flexible pipes, not of metal.

18. Leather and imitations of leather, and goods made of these materials and not included in other classes; animal skins, hides; trunks and traveling bags; umbrellas, parasols and walking sticks; whips, harness and saddlery.

19. Building materials (non-metallic); nonmetallic rigid pipes for building; asphalt, pitch and bitumen; nonmetallic transportable buildings; monuments, not of metal.
20. Furniture, mirrors, picture frames; goods (not included in other classes) of wood, cork, reed, cane, wicker, horn, bone, ivory, whalebone, shell, amber, mother-of-pearl, meerschaum and substitutes for all these materials, or of plastics.
21. Household or kitchen utensils and containers (not of precious metal or coated therewith); combs and sponges; brushes (except paint brushes); brush-making materials; articles for cleaning purposes; steel-wool; un-worked or semi-worked glass (except glass used in building); glassware, porcelain and earthenware not included in other classes.
22. Ropes, string, nets, tents, awnings, tarpaulins, sails, sacks and bags (not included in other classes); padding and stuffing materials (except of rubber or plastics); raw fibrous textile materials.
23. Yarns and threads, for textile use.
24. Textiles and textile goods, not included in other classes; beds and table covers.
25. Clothing, footwear, headgear.
26. Lace and embroidery, ribbons and braid; buttons, hooks and eyes, pins and needles; artificial flowers.
27. Carpets, rugs, mats and matting, linoleum and other materials for covering existing floors; wall hangings (non-textile).
28. Games and playthings; gymnastic and sporting articles not included in other classes; decorations for Christmas trees.
29. Meat, fish, poultry and game; meat extracts; preserved, dried and cooked fruits and vegetables; jellies, jams, fruit sauces; eggs, milk and milk products; edible oils and fats.
30. Coffee, tea, cocoa, sugar, rice, tapioca, sago, artificial coffee; flour and preparations made from cereals, bread, pastry and confectionery, ices; honey, treacle; yeast, baking powder; salt, mustard; vinegar, sauces (condiments); spices; ice.
31. Agricultural, horticultural and forestry products and grains not included in other classes; live animals; fresh fruits and vegetables; seeds, natural plants and flowers; foodstuffs for animals; malt.
32. Beers; mineral and aerated waters and other nonalcoholic drinks; fruit drinks and fruit juices; syrups and other preparations for making beverages.
33. Alcoholic beverages (except beers).
34. Tobacco; smokers' articles; matches.

SERVICES

35. Advertising; business management; business administration; office functions.
36. Insurance; financial affairs; monetary affairs; real estate affairs.
37. Building construction; repair; installation services.
38. Telecommunications.
39. Transport; packaging and storage of goods; travel arrangement
40. Treatment of materials.
41. Education; providing of training; entertainment; sporting and cultural activities.
42. Scientific and technological services and research and design relating thereto; industrial analysis and research services; design and development of computer hardware and software; legal services.
43. Services for providing food and drink; temporary accommodations.
44. Medical services; veterinary services; hygienic and beauty care for human beings or animals; agriculture, horticulture and forestry services.
45. Personal and social services rendered by others to meet the needs of individuals; security services for the protection of property and individuals.

END OF TRADEMARK MINI LESSON

Some Quick Copyright Basics

Other factors to be considered when creating your identity is taking ownership of everything you produce in terms of written, audio and video related material. Did you: 1) create innovative marketing materials, 2) create a website from scratch with an innovative look or arrangement, 3) create materials such as a line of books or training materials, 4) did you create interesting character drawings that will be in a book or advertising campaign that you want to be able to prove came out of your head? **What do I mean?** Go see what Warner Bros., Disney, Nick and all of the companies with cartoon type characters do. They immediately lock them down with Copyrights and Trademarks. Why, because they will make millions of dollars by licensing out those characters for placement on everything you can imagine. Things you create have value and you must assert your rights to those things that you create. If you don't, don't cry but there are plenty of people who will gladly take your concept if there is money to be made. Another thing to consider is that when you first create something that is copyrightable or trademark worthy you may not initially realize the immense value of what you have come up with. Did the Harry Potter author know she would be worth a billion dollars?

When it comes to copyright, all of the information from instructions to forms will be found at **http://www.copyright.gov/register**. Gone are all of the separate forms for each separate category such as Form TX which was used for Literary vs. audio vs. video, etc. All forms have now been condensed into the new and improved Form **CO for Paper Filings** and **Form eCO** for the On-Line Filings. Copyrights are not hard to do. You make your determination as to what type of copyright filing it is. Is it literary, sound recordings, art, is it a published work, it is an unpublished work. **On the site they offer a great tutorial**. Just to let you know, you pay the fee before you fill out everything unlike the Trademark filing where you put the filing together then pay the fee. Just take your time and read everything. It is important to note that you now have two choices as to how to file. If you choose to file on-line then the fee will be $35.00. If you choose to file by mail the fee will be $45.00. Have your documents, pictures, recordings etc. ready to go in an easy to find area on your computer. For a compilation, make sure you have everything together in a PDF file and make sure that each separate piece of the compilation has a cover sheet that identifies each separate section plus a table of contents in the front so that the items included in the compilation are clearly identified.

Again, as with your Trademark, you have to protect your property before you go ahead and send your work or your concept to people who you may not know that well. How are you going to prove that the things you send to others or show to others is your work? By filing the copyright when your concepts are in a form that necessitates that you do; this will help to show that your work is recorded in the copyright office and can be retrieved at any time. You will receive a registration number from the copyright office that identifies that work. It holds more weight than you screaming that someone took your writings, pictures, sounds, movies and used them without your permission.

For those of you who are script writers who wish to protect your scripts **you can file a copyright** but you can also go to the **WGAW registry**. The WGAW registry is the official script and screenplay registration service of **The Writers Guild of America**. The WGA Registry assists writers and other creators in establishing the completion dates of material written for the fields of radio, film, television, and interactive media. Think about doing this as well. **For example**: You send a script out to some individual or company and 1 of 3 things occurs. They are the following: 1) You never hear from them again. You follow-up and they don't ever respond, 2) You hear from them but they say that it does not quite fit what they are looking for and 3) Either they never respond or they say it is not for them but a year or two later you now see your movie concept on television or in the movies. That is why each and every script or work you do should be filed so that you have proof that an idea was yours and you can prove it. **Number everything** you send out with a particular numbering system such as 0001, 0002 etc. and 1) record where **each** numbered script, book etc. was sent to, 2) the date it was sent, 3) the company or individual it went to, 4) the way it was sent, (email or by regular mail). There are services you can use that tell you when the recipient opens the email. Even MS Word Outlook has a setting to let you know when it has been opened.

IMPORTANT: It may also be a very good idea if sending a paper copy or electronic copy of anything you send to anyone who wants to see your project to use a **watermark** on the document whether you initially generate the watermark in **MS Word** or you can place the watermark in the Adobe PDF file when you convert the file from MS Word over to Adobe PDF.

Adobe Professional lets you create a watermark in the PDF file so does Nuance. The watermark lies under the text in another layer. Those who have skills **can remove your PDF watermark. They do so because they want to take your stuff and they don't want to compensate you NOR GIVE YOU CREDIT!** So, another great tip is to create the watermark in the PDF file then convert the entire PDF file over to JPG pictures and then convert all the JPEG pictures back to PDF. In this way, the **watermark becomes intertwined with the text and they cannot remove it.** I know that there are plenty of good people out there who are sincere but we are not worried about them. We do need to be aware of the others.

What they will have to do to get rid of your mark, is to totally **retype** the document **from scratch** so make it **a pain in the rear** for them. You can place the name of your company, the name of the project or whatever you deem as your watermark. The watermark should not obscure the text and it should be light enough so as to not be hard to read, but **dark enough**, so anyone can see it even if they use a copier it will still appear. Hey, I worked in top-tier law firms for 22 years. Take it from me, I know what I am talking about in relation to document production.

Finally, **don't think** that a major firm **does not have very tight control** over their intellectual property and so should you. If you are sloppy when it comes to ideas, you will be burned.

Film people and screen writers please check out www.wgawregistry.org

I think that we can all agree that before we go asking for money for a project that we should have taken steps concerning the trademark, patent and copyright aspect. At least if you have filed 1 of the 3 or all of the 3 depending on the nature of your situation, it shows that the project will have Intellectual Property value and you had the presence of mind to protect it. Remember, the paper napkin guys are going to make money people cringe. They want to see that you have the mindset of a businessman. They don't want a guy who came up with an idea and he is basically asking for money but has no structure or game plan and no identity. Don't get me wrong. **I applaud anyone who works hard every day and comes up with good ideas but in the game of money and getting concepts off the ground, you have to look the part in terms of your business set up** so if you are basic and new to the whole world of inventing or business development, take the time to develop your sophistication. You can learn anything that anyone else can learn. You will be that much more comfortable and aware of everything if you do.

Domain Names:

Again, when talking about identity, you are going to want to lock up a domain name that represents your company and the website. People are going to want to know that you have a website (even an introductory site). People do not like to see the words "**Under Construction**" when they look up your site. Do yourself a favor, do not make the site public until it is ready to be viewed. So having a domain name under your control and a website is an important item to have done before you seek money or open for business.

Now, some of you may say, what if I am working on a project that I want to keep under wraps? I totally understand this concern. What you can do is to establish a site that initially is **general in nature** and talks about the industry. You don't necessarily have to tell the world hey, this is exactly what I am up to. You don't even have to activate the site right away. But, if you do, **the idea is that you have an entire structure in place as to your initial presence using the name of your invention, corporation or product name etc. and this is going to go a long way in terms of how someone who is in the money business or a would be customer looks at you**. What you are trying **not to do** is having a website that uses one name, a Facebook page with another name, a Twitter account with still another name and a Skype account with still another name. That will only result in people being confused as to the identity of the entity you are trying to create. This is all about putting the beginning structure in place and establishing a clear identity. You can secure your domain name and there are many website template programs that will enable you to work on them undercover and only when you are ready to show them, will you then connect your domain name to the homepage of the website and make it public. I will discuss this in the up coming paragraph.

Some thoughts about domain names.

Let's talk about the domain name aspect. You know that when you start a business you need to have a domain name. You will need a website because people sort of take it for granted that you should have one if you are running a business. So, where do we go to purchase a domain name? There are many places that sell domain names and I usually go to Godaddy.com because I like their customer service. Some people host from **the same company** that they buy their domain name from. You don't necessarily have to, not at all.

Now, If you buy a domain name from company A and you hook up with a website hosting company which I will call company B, you can point your domain name residing on the server of one hosting company to the server location of another hosting company using the forward feature of the service you bought the domain name from. As for me, I usually buy my domain name on godaddy.com and I point my domain name to the home page of my **freewebs.com** site or my **weebly.com** site. Both freewebs.com and weebly.com are very easy to use sites that anybody can quickly use to create a nice web presence. No, it is not a sophisticated portal but it most certainly will do the job of a basic but thorough website. They both have links for social media, for youtube.com, for Twitter.com, for blogs, for photo albums, for document downloads etc. These sites are free and if you want to pay a small monthly fee to add even more functionality, you can simply purchase a package that may cost you $50.00 or so for the entire year. It is amazing what you can do with these free sites in terms of the look. Domain name buying tip: Before you buy your domain go to fatwallet.com. Look up godaddy.com and you will find many coupons for initial domain buying which will give you a nice 20-30% discount on the overall domain name price.

So we go to godaddy.com in order to look up our proposed domain name.

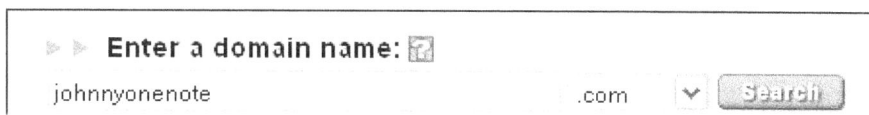

-

- I put in my proposed name and pray.....

✓ JOHNNYONENOTE.COM is available!

Okay: **Now it gets interesting**! If you look at the top of this picture it says that **johnnyonenote.com is available**. Okay great! It also alerts you to the other extensions that are also available under that name. We recommend that you grab as many of the open domains that you can afford under your proposed name. Maybe the **.US, .BIZ, .INFO, .NET, .MOBI, .TV and .Org** This will cost you a little money but not that much in reality. This will serve to protect you against other people using your proposed name by purchasing one of these other domain extensions that use your name. The idea here is that you want to stop **others** from profiting on your name by using your name and simply using a different extension of the name.

What if a rival does something underhanded such as putting out a site that says how you wronged them or how your product is bad or your service inadequate using an extension that you could have easily purchased so that **it was not available** for this purpose. This would then leave you frustrated that you just didn't buy those URL's when you had the chance. People can damage your proposed name and reputation before you really even get started. This is all about locking up your name in the internet world and this is a vital step that we do for ourselves and anyone else that we deal with in terms of our business services. It is also noteworthy that **.US** is for the United States and any trademark owner should own and has the right to own the **.US** URL extension of the trademark they own.

Note: If you look up a proposed domain name that you want and find that it is already secured by someone else, you may wish to know who actually owns the name and when they bought it. Every web hosting company has a place on their site called **"WHO IS"**. The **Who Is** database will let you know 1) who they are, (provided that they did not subscribe to a domain name proxy service that protects the name and address of the actual owner) 2) where they are from, 3) when they bought the domain and 4) when it expires. You may wish to keep track and see if that person renews the domain. If not, you can at that point make the attempt to purchase it. Our advice is do not let any one name hang you up and stop your progress. Some people who buy URL's also purchase the proxy service that protects a person from knowing the actual name and address of the owner of the domain name. If you have a business where you don't want to have someone find out your personal address you owe it to yourself to use the **Domains By Proxy** service when you purchase your domains. There is an additional fee for this service but privacy is very important to certain individuals that do not want to have people knocking on their door unexpectedly. If you have a site where your picture is posted on the site and you live at the place indicated in the **"Who Is"** listing, you should consider the **proxy service** for your protection and privacy.

Any photos you place on your website that show you in them should first be stripped of the location information especially if you took the photos using a digital phone camera. MS Word has a feature to take out this info and all cell phones give you the opportunity to turn of the tracking feature. You don't want to have people knowing where you are especially if they have a problem with you or are just plain crazy.

Once you buy your domain, you will have your name which can now be forwarded to the home page of your web hosting provider if you are not hosting from the same company you bought the domain name from. Finally, **establish the email accounts that go along with your newly purchased domain name**. You can do that from godaddy.com immediately after purchasing your domain name. So, if for example your new domain is easygrow.com then immediately do louis@easygrow.com, info@easygrow.com, products@easygrow.com etc.

Social Media:

Facebook:

Slowly but surely we are quietly creating a presence for our new venture. Now, let us talk about the social media aspect. Yes, you can go and create a Facebook page. If you are initially working on a product that is still under wraps then like I told you earlier, talk about things in general that are already in the public domain. There is no law that says that as soon as I establish a website or a Facebook page that I have to immediately tell the world all of my secrets and plans.

No, you don't. You need to be quiet until everything is in place. Talk about the state of the industry that you are in, tell people where they can find you in terms of email, Skype, phone etc. Answer some questions. Write an industry related article or two. Blog back and forth with the people who connect with you. The time will come when you totally let everyone know exactly what you are doing. Your goal at first is to establish the social media presence **QUICKLY** and **QUIETLY** so that you are not in a position of scrambling to get these things done or accidentally alerting others to what you are doing so that they grab the social media name before you. If you go around telling everyone what you are doing, don't be shocked that when you go to secure your Twitter name, your Facebook name, your Pinterest name or other social media related name that someone already took it. People can be spiteful and don't think that it does not happen. Two things to always think about which is **the crab in a barrel** and **the stab in the back**. The crab in a barrel occurs when certain people see you trying to get ahead and they grab you right back into the barrel just as you were about to be free. The stab in the back is the individual who says how great it is to hear about your new venture only to be acting on your new venture in order to take advantage of it before you can even get going. Thanks to my friend Cassandra who pointed out to me the crab in a barrel people. Once you know the concept, you will come across the situation often.

Your Facebook page can act as a mini-hub that in a snap shot lets people know all about what you do and your service and serves to provide links to where they can buy your products and services. Those products can be produced materials, books, audios, videos, affiliate orientated connections that you have as well as keeping people abreast with what you are up to and what you are going to be offering in the coming months.

If you go to **Amazon or half.com** you can get a basic book for almost nothing (used) on establishing your Facebook page which will save you significant time and money. Of course, if you have the budget you can always hire someone to do your Facebook page. College kids are a good source because they are very tech savvy but they will take a little less to do a good job for you.

On your Facebook page you can list the following other social media connections,

Twitter:

Set up your **Twitter.com** account. Keep it quiet. Start following people in your industry. The time will come when you push to have them follow you but you want to follow others at first. See what they are up to. Make a few of your own generalized Tweets. The good thing is that **your name is secure as a Twitter handle**. Again, there are some really inexpensive and free books and great info on Twitter.com itself on how to best utilize their service. Same for Pinerest. We are trying to get everything secure and in place without alerting your would-be competition who may intentionally do something stupid in order to block you or to make your life difficult in getting established. *Stealth presence building* *is essential at first.* Sooner than you think you will be exclaiming to the world what you have to offer.

LinkedIn:

This is an important piece to the puzzle because as you will see, LinkedIn can be an additional and valuable form of exposure. It can be a very nice extension to your **website**, to your **Facebook** page, and any other social media page. Go to LinkedIn and create a thorough profile. This profile can act as an electronic business card. Your LinkedIn profile link can be placed on your social media pages, your business card as well as your website.

Let people know what you do and who you are. No need to tell them **at this point** about your new business or project. If you have a new service that a lot of other people already have such as a banker, a lawyer, a business owner, etc., then I see no major problem. If you have **a new invention** or other new (disruptive) business model, then I would not be revealing anything until you can get yourself funded. You need to do this by having a meeting and pitching your product to a select group of people who are in the business of venture capital or hard money. Don't ever do it by telling everyone publicly what you are doing because you will lose your advantage. Your competition can now be working on the very thing that you thought was so unique and had worked so hard for. Don't hand anything away. That really would be foolish. The trick is to come out of nowhere so that your competition is totally taken by surprise. Bringing a new idea or product to the market place is difficult enough. Don't give anything away. Getting things in place is getting things in place. Getting ready to open for business will go into effect when your identity is in place and secure.

Whether you are a small company or a large company, having a LinkedIn presence will be a great addition to you **building your initial presence and the creation of your identity as a new business**.

I am not talking about just going on LinkedIn and creating a profile. That is very helpful, but I am talking about going on LinkedIn and creating a **Group of your own** for your company or genre. By creating a group of your own, you can control the articles and information that you disseminate. You are in charge of what goes out. On my group, "Entrepreneurs and Inventors Welcome", I constantly post great information having to do with tools, issues and tricks of the trade as to entrepreneurial day to day things. I have also maintained a large group **"AdvanceTo Legal Word Processing Training"** where people come to my group for MS Word related information and training. What a wonderful boost to my credibility as a teacher and consultant. I also make it my business to constantly be pushing my offerings. So, I may write an article, whereby it is very useful information, and at the end of the article, I place my website and a short mini-commercial for the thing I am pushing at the moment.   No matter what you do, you have something to offer and creating your own group is a wonderful way to create a presence.

Besides you having your own group, **you are allowed to join 50 groups in LinkedIn for free**. So, if you join at least 10 other groups from your line of business, you can take part in their discussions, tell people about your group and expand your reach to other people. Lend your expertise; solve a problem or two for people in other groups. Give them a reason to take note of you and want to see more of you. Remember, you will come across groups that have 10,000 and 50,000 followers, so if you place an article or a comment that makes people take notice, this is major exposure. **By participating in this process, you are causing people to take notice of you, to look up your profile, to check out or join your group and to check out or buy something from your website or ask for your services**. Having your own group and taking part as a whole gives you more credibility since many people from all over the world will be exposed to you. The majority of these people most probably would have never heard of you if not for your involvement on LinkedIn. This goes a long way as to our plan to quietly establish our presence while working behind the scenes for our new innovative venture. **People can get to know you and see what your core knowledge is way before you even come out in full force concerning your new project or business.** Remember, Facebook, is very good for business exposure but the business of LinkedIn is business and you cannot go wrong by making your presence known.

A couple of strategies you may wish to consider concerning LinkedIn. If you wish to talk to someone who posted something that was of interest to you for possible business, then I would do the following: If you reply to their post do it either by asking them to **accept you as a contact** so you may talk to them privately through LinkedIn or at the location in the group of their posting choose the **"Reply Privately"** choice.

I say this because if you reply **publicly** to the person then everyone in that group is going to know exactly what is going on. If you had the chance to corner this individual, to talk to them privately so you may do business, doing it publicly will cause many people to latch onto that person thus diverting them with phony and/or fishing expeditions and taking away the opportunity with the person you were hoping to do some business with and thus ruining the opportunity. **When they do contact you privately, always request their email, phone number and Skype number if they have it.   The email will put you in position to be able to send documents back and forth**. Skype will help you if they are in a foreign country and you are in the states and you want to be able to pick up the phone and talk or instant message them.

I would respond to a LinkedIn post in my group or another group I am connected to **PUBLICLY**, when I **INTENTIONALLY** want other people to see what I am asking for or informing others about areas that I can assist with. Then, this causes others who are selling or looking for that same certain service or item to reach out to me in mass so it serves a role to go public and thus receive many offers for the same service or item.

Now, let us talk about Skype. Yes I know you are just putting together your presence. Skype is going to instantly give you the ability to talk with people anywhere in the world without having to pay absorbent fees for the actual service. I use my "free" account all the time. You can either call them on your Skype account or you can instant message people back and forth. If someone such as a potential supplier, business associate, backer, joint venture person etc. wants to talk with you and they are in a foreign country the easiest and most effective way to do so is through your Skype account that you can have on your desktop or your smart phone. Again, you want to make sure you **secure the Skype name that is in sync with the name of your company or your new invention or your new business concept name**. In other words, don't do a Skype name such as Joe 46. Be professional and keep consistent with all of these different tools that are allowing you to establish a presence.

Another really good thing about Skype, is that when we go back and forth with the instant message feature, I can then take that transcript and I can send it to someone else to inform them and elaborate as to how my conversation unfolded since the transcript will show the back and forth question and answer. It should be noted that if the subject matter was of a personal and/or private nature, you should not send that transcript to anyone else.

Note: What I would **not** do is the following. Do not participate or put together a conference call on **Skype**. If you are in the middle of negotiating some deal or you are trying to broker a deal and you want to protect your buyer or seller connection **Skype** is **not** the way to do so. Everyone on the Skype conference call will now know everyone else on that call since all of the Skype names taking part will be visible to everyone. Now, the other side knows everyone from your side and in many cases they will now go directly to them and cut you out of the deal. **Use Skype on a one to one basis unless of course you are all working on the same deal from your side.**

Free Conference Call International.

This is an important piece as well. If you look at everything that we have discussed thus far, you can start to see the structure of your company presence starting to take shape. By doing all of these things you are taking control of the proposed business, invention or new device name fully.

For Conference Calls, make use of **Freeconferencecall.Com, Freeconferencecallinternational.com** and **simpletollfree.com**. Free Conference Call gives you the ability at any time to have numerous people all dial into the same number. You also get free screen sharing and people can see you if you want them to. You get a **dial in number** and a **passcode**. The free service records the call if you wish and gives you the ability to hand out a number that allows your customers or clients to dial in and hear the already recorded and finished call. The **International Free Conference Call** from the same company gives your clients the ability to call **a local number** from a vast listing of available countries while all of you still use **the same pass code** to get on the call. And still another service from Free Conference Call -- **Simple Toll Free**, allows you to give your clients and customers an 800 number to dial into for conferences and **allows you to download the finished call and post it on your site** or make a **Pod Cast** of it. Simple way to make cheap commercials or interviews. They charge 6 cents a minute per conference call participant but you have an 800 number.

Note: If at all possible, when you participate in conference calls, push heartily for your **conference call number** and **passcode** to be used for the call. The reason for this is that after the call, the owner of the conference call number (hopefully you), will receive an email showing **all of the numbers that dialed in for that conference call**. So, just like the situation in Skype, the other side will now have all of your contacts in terms of their phone numbers and locations and in many situations can then use that info to bypass you or to get to talk to people that you did not want them to have ready access to. So, keep this in mind for it will come up again and again. That is the reason why you should have your own dial in number at the ready. **Many people list their Free Conference Call number and passcode in the footer of their email after their regular number**. So, if a situation comes up, those in your loop already have your conference call number since they have an email of yours. Push to have them use your conference number and pass code if you could.

You Tube:

Create a **Youtube.com account**. Establish your **You Tube channel**. In your channel, you can do mini commercials for your product, service or device. You can do PowerPoint and Camtasia like presentations that talk about the industry, about what you are doing. If you are still in the middle of getting protected by a Trademark or Patent you can still establish a presence that shows people the knowledge that you do have within the genre that you work in. Having a nice established Youtube.com channel will enable you to place links within your videos so people can be directed to your website to either purchase something or obtain more information. These same videos get indexed into the search engines such as Google so it is a good idea to establish this presence.

The videos that you do produce, will not go to waste because they can be used within blogs, within emails, within social media (Facebook etc.) so having the You Tube channel will help you to establish a presence. If you do your research there are many screen capture programs that enable you to do narration while you show something on the screen as well as provided video of you talking directly to your audience. I suggest you have fun with the whole thing. If I were you check out Maria Andros at mariaandros.com. She is a business strategy and video marketing expert and you will learn a lot from her. If you wish to sell videos that you produce, you can use Amazon's Create Space and there are many other services that allow you to upload your videos and people then have to purchase them in order to get a streaming video of the information. But, for straight up commercials YouTube is the way to go on your own YouTube channel.

Radioguestlist.com

This is another one of those freebies that can help to get you exposure and make some good connections. Most of the people who advertise their radio shows are doing podcasts but these are great ways to gain experience. I have been on numerous radio shows and you get better and better with each one. You sign up with them and then they send to your email each day a number of radio interview opportunities. You look at the subject matter of the radio shows featured that day to see if any fit your subject matter. If so,. you follow up with the program director or booking person for that show.

Have a Radio Bio Sheet ready and that will help you as well. Put down some history about yourself, what you do, what you bring to the table and why you would make a great guest. If you wrote a book you may even include a sample chapter or two so that they get a feel of your style of writing. If they are interested they will contact you and they will tell you how to go about booking yourself for the interview. They usually run about 15 to 30 minutes tops. Prepare for the interview so that you have a lot of good stuff to offer the audience. It is also a good idea to have some success stories as well.

Incorporation:

Incorporation is a very important piece of the puzzle. When it comes to incorporation, you do not have to necessarily name your corporation with the name of your device, product or business concept name. You can name your corporation anything that you feel is a good umbrella feel to the overall work and genre that you are in. So, if I have a line of clothing called **Cool Sun** (as I do) I can have a corporation named **IDesign (which I had)**. No matter what you decide to name your corporation, I believe that it will look very good to have a corporation in place with a bank account associated with it before you start your fund raising or opening the door for business. It will definitely give you a bit more of sophistication which I believe will help. You want people to have to make out a check to your company name rather than you personally. You will have a bank officer associated with you, you have a ready Swift Code, Routing and Bank Account if you are in a venture and need to be paid by wire transfer, you will have access to business lines of credit as well so the corporation is a must to help you in building your credibility with your new venture. It will also give you protection for you personally, and will provide you with some good tax write-offs for expenses you incur having to do with putting your company together from scratch. Some more information regarding corporations. Keep in mind that I am giving you general information based on the fact that I live in New York.

How do you check if the name is available for incorporation?

You can check on your own state website for this information. Every state has its own official state website. As a business owner, I live in New York and use the "Official New York State Website", which will be used as an example: In your state look up Official Texas State Website, Official Florida State Website etc. you will get all of the information you need as it relates to incorporating and searching out already create corporations. In this way you can check that your proposed name is available.

- http://www.dos.state.ny.us/corp/corpwww.html

CORPORATIONS AND BUSINESS ENTITIES

- Mission
- Search Our Corporation-Business Entity Database Here
- Rules and Regulations of the Division of Corporations
- Legal Memoranda
  Doing Business in New York
  Formation of Business Entities

  FREQUENTLY ASKED QUESTIONS
  Business Corporations
  Not-for-Profit Corporations
  Limited Liability Companies
  Limited Partnerships
  Limited Liability Partnerships
  Biennial Statements for Corporations and LLCs and LLP Statement
  Updates for LLPs

  FILING INFORMATION, FORMS AND FEES
  Business Corporations
  Not-for-Profit Corporations
  Limited Liability Companies
  Limited Partnerships
  Limited Liability Partnerships

- Mission
- Search Our Corporation-Business Entity Database Here
- Rules and Regulations of the Division of Corporations
- Legal Memoranda

In the New York State site they have an area as shown above that has everything you could possibly do as it relates to incorporation. The "Search Our Corporation Database" section is important because this is where you get the chance to see if your proposed name is available. If you put your proposed name in and it comes up, then someone else has already secured that name. If that is the case don't be discouraged. Sometimes it is a sign from above that you should think of **another name** and many times (and it has happened to me) you end up coming up with an even **better** name than before.

Next, what type of corporation are you going to going to be? There are C-Corps Limited Liability Corps., Sub Chapter S Corps., Personal Corps., Not-for-Profit Corps. and many more. Once you decide upon your name, you would go to the part of the site in your state that provides the automated/mail in/fax in process to create your corporation. At the same site, as part of the overall process, you can also receive your new Tax I.D. (Identification Number) that same day as well as your **certificate of incorporation**, which you can print as well. Once you get your **certificate of incorporation** you can go to the bank with your **black book** (must have the black book), a loose leaf binder containing the *minutes, by-*

Laws, customized Stock certificates, stock transfer ledger and of course your Certificate of Incorporation..

You can go to one of the many services that will prepare a Black Book. Your **Black Book** would include your **Certificate of Incorporation**, meeting forms, transfer of ownership of stock forms, etc. With your Certificate of Incorporation and your black book you would then open your **Corporate bank account**. You might even at this point try to establish a line of credit for your new corporation by applying to one of the many credit card companies. The bank account will give your new company much needed credibility. When people want to pay you for your services they will now be making the checks out to **your company name**.

The forms area of whatever state you live in will look somewhat similar in nature to the New York site. You just have to remember that you must go to **your** Official State Site!

FILING INFORMATION, FORMS AND FEES
Business Corporations
Not-for-Profit Corporations
Limited Liability Companies
Limited Partnerships
Limited Liability Partnerships

As promised, here are the different types of corporations and their meanings:

The following appeared on the **New York State website, Division of Corporations** link where a full explanation is given as to the differences between the different types of corporate entities that exist. This will be very helpful in having you see the **distinction** between the different types of corporations.

If you want to operate a **business corporation:**

- then you must *file* a Certificate of Incorporation (signed by at least one incorporator) *with* the Department of State.
- Personal liability is limited, for shareholders.
- The life-span of the business is perpetual; *or* for a designated period stipulated in the Certificate of Incorporation.
- For purposes of taxation a corporation pays state franchise taxes and taxes on income; shareholders pay taxes on income distributed as dividends (a limited exception exists for "Subchapter S" corporations). When it comes to Subchapter S corporations they are allowed to pass their losses though to the individual, so that they reduce their personal income. Subchapter S corporations were created in order to assist smaller corporations (with no more

than 75 owners) the ability to off-set their losses against other income.

If you want to operate a **limited liability company:**

- then you must *file* Articles of Organization (signed by one or more organizers) *with* the Department of State.
- Personal liability is generally limited, although the Articles of Organization can specify that member(s) will be liable for company debts, etc.
- The life-span of the business may be for a designated period stipulated in the Articles of Organization; *or* until a dissolution event occurs and the company takes no action to continue.
- For purposes of taxation an LLC can elect its classification for federal tax purposes. An LLC with two or more members can elect to be an association (corporation) or a partnership; an LLC with one member can elect to be an association (corporation) or elect to be disregarded as an entity separate from its owner (in effect, to be treated as a sole proprietorship for federal tax purposes).

If you want to operate a **general partnership:**

- then you must *file* an Assumed Name Certificate (following an agreement of the partners) *with* the clerk of the county/ies in which the business is conducted.
- Personal liability is joint and individual for the general partners who are responsible for the obligations of the partnership.
- The life-span of the business is for a designated period stipulated in the partnership agreement; *or* until a dissolution event occurs.
- For purposes of taxation a general partnership is not treated as a separate taxable entity; business income is taxed through each general partner's personal tax return.

If you want to operate a **limited partnership:**

- then you must *file* a Certificate of Limited Partnership (following an agreement of the partners) *with* the Department of State.
- Personal liability is joint and individual for the general partners who are responsible for the obligations of the partnership; limited partners are liable to the extent of their capital contribution to the partnership.

The life-span of the business is for a designated period stipulated in the partnership agreement; *or* until a dissolution event occurs, subject to any right to continue that may be stated in the partnership agreement. The life span of the business might involve for example, a project that will last two years and after the period stated concerning this project is over then the partnership is no longer in effect.

- For purposes of taxation a limited partnership is not treated as a separate taxable entity; business income is taxed through each partner's personal tax return.

If you want to operate a **sole proprietorship**:

- then you must *file* an Assumed Name Certificate *with* the clerk of the county/ies in which the business is conducted *ONLY IF* you are operating under a name other than the proprietor's (no formation document is required).
- Personal liability is full- a sole proprietor is personally responsible for all debts of his or her business.
- The life-span of the business is determined by the individual (proprietorships automatically cease on the retirement or death of the sole proprietor).
- For purposes of taxation business income is reported and taxed through the sole proprietor's personal tax return.'

Important: Registered Agent. You do not have to incorporate in your state. Depending on the tax implications you may opt to incorporate in another state other than the one in which you live. There is nothing wrong with this. If you are to incorporate within a state that you do not live in then you must use a **Registered Agent** in the state in which you incorporate. The Registered Agent will provide you with a **business address** within the state that you incorporated. They will cost around $100.00 per year but you now have an **official address** where legal papers can be sent to and other official information that would need to be sent to your official corporate address. The Registered Agents for each state are listed in the Incorporation area of the state's official website that you incorporated in.

......*

Your Executive Summary

This is not a full fledged business plan by any means but it can act as a mini business plan or a really good snap shot of what you are trying to do. It is good to have this ready for someone who asks to have a company profile like document. The Executive Summary can be focused on an opportunity but it can also be one that can gives a very good overview of what your new venture or service is about. Things that can go into the plan are the nature of the business or service, the team involved in the venture, what you are looking to accomplish in the industry. A snapshot as to what you bring to the table that will have you stand out opposed to the entities that are already out there in your line of business. All of your contact information. You can be very inventive with these if you take the time with them but it is a nice touch to have a company profile/executive summary at the ready **after you have established and secured all of your intellectual property and social media**.

The sample below was done for a patent that I was working on but depending on your company type you can see how you can use the Executive Summary as a mini business plan, extended mini-website, business card, company profile and on and on. Take a look at what I used it for and then see how you can use the concept in your venture.

LOUIS® INTERACTIVE
Executive Summary
[A site to remember]
US Patent No.:7,577,602
TRADEMARK REGISTRATION NUMBER 3385848
Copyright 2014 © by Louis Ellman

Contact Information
Louis Corporation
Louis Ellman, President
louis@advanceto.com
888-422-0692 Ext. 2
Anywhere Avenue
Any City, State Zip
LawFirm: YOUR LAW FIRM,
located in City of Law Firm,
New York

Business Description:

The Mission of this corporation is to be the catalyst and liaison between the ▉▉▉▉ Companies, ▉▉▉▉ and ▉▉▉ Companies. The three industries need to work in conjunction for the purpose of giving people the opportunity to *easily secure* ▉▉▉▉ related directly to an ▉▉▉▉ for ▉▉▉▉. A "▉▉▉▉" is all that is needed to ensure that you don't lose out on an opportunity.

1.   Here is the top portion of the executive summary. **Note:** A) I placed the name of the company, B) the patent number associated with it, C) my trademark registration number and D) I am claiming copyright for the textual portion of the executive summary. You may not have your patent or trademark at the time of writing your executive summary but you may have them pending or somewhere along the chronology and you can put that information down. In the tan area to the left note that I have placed 1) my contact information, 2) my title, 3) my address and 4) the name of the law firm that I am using or plan to use. Under "**Business Description**", I tried to put in a nice concise mini-summary of the proposed business.

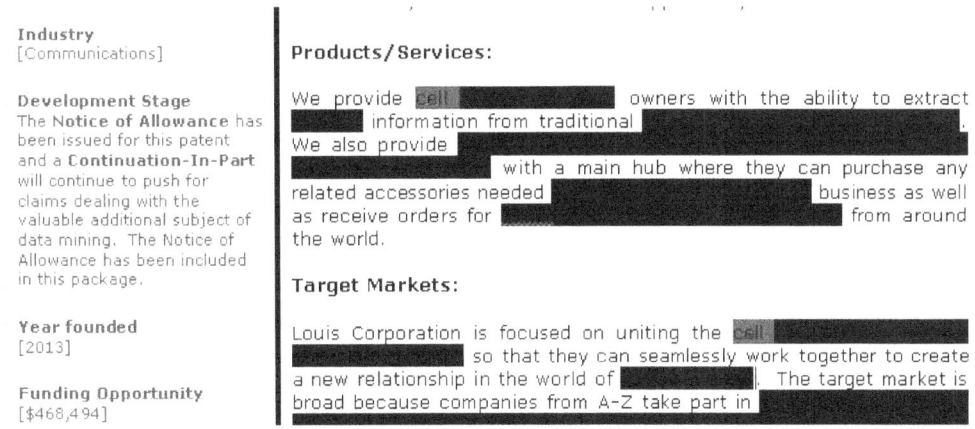

Industry
[Communications]

Development Stage
The Notice of Allowance has been issued for this patent and a **Continuation-In-Part** will continue to push for claims dealing with the valuable additional subject of data mining. The Notice of Allowance has been included in this package.

Year founded
[2013]

Funding Opportunity
[$468,494]

Products/Services:

We provide ▉▉▉ ▉▉▉▉▉▉ owners with the ability to extract ▉▉▉▉ information from traditional ▉▉▉▉. We also provide ▉▉▉▉ with a main hub where they can purchase any related accessories needed ▉▉▉▉ business as well as receive orders for ▉▉▉▉ from around the world.

Target Markets:

Louis Corporation is focused on uniting the ▉▉▉ ▉▉▉▉ ▉▉▉▉ so that they can seamlessly work together to create a new relationship in the world of ▉▉▉▉. The target market is broad because companies from A-Z take part in ▉▉▉▉

2.   So moving right along, we have the "**Products/Services**" section and a short paragraph on the "**Target Markets**" that your new device, patent or service will serve. If you look to the tan area on the left we have a title called "**Industry**" followed by another title called "**Developmental Stage**". If you notice in this area, for this particular executive summary, that I gave them up to date information concerning the issuance of my patent for the device that I was seeking funds for at the time. We then have a title called "**Year Founded**" and you can put the year you were incorporated if you are incorporated. The title "**Funding Opportunity**" you will put the total amount of money you are seeking. Then underneath, you do a short synopsis (breakdown) of what you are going to be using the money for.

Use of Funds
$100,000 Product Development
$225,000 Marketing/Sales
$18,030 Domain and TM Protection
$4,000 Worldwide Affiliate Program
$50,000 Licensing agreements for Trademark Use
$25,000 for Travel

Existing Investors
The Process has begun.

large corporations will want to use this medium.

Strategy/Barriers To Entry:

Louis Corporation plans to enter the clothing ▮▮▮▮▮ by developing affiliate relationships that bring business to those entities instead of being in competition with them. Since our ▮▮▮▮▮ will be programmed to work with all ▮▮▮▮, we are giving the consumer immediate access to use the technology for their own business ventures as well as benefiting from ▮▮▮▮▮ that other ▮▮▮▮▮. We plan to replicate the system in as many countries as possible by making foreign contacts through U.S. Partners. Patent applications have been granted to protect core technology and Trademarks are already in place.

Customers:

The ▮▮▮▮▮
▮▮▮▮▮
who receive orders that stem from our site, as well as signage companies who receive orders that stem from our site. The customer base really cuts across the three industries (the ▮▮▮▮

3.   Moving right along, we have a title called "**Strategy/Barriers To Entry**". Here, you will attempt to summarize how you enter the market and how you can overcome any hurdles. You also want to show how you plan to do it smoothly and express your idea of how you will enter the market in the most cost efficient way that affords the least amount of resistance to you and your wallet (in essence, your strategy). Next, we have the "**Customers**" section and you can identify what you feel is the profile of your would-be customer. In the tan section to the left, we have the very important "**Use of Funds**" section where you do a quick breakdown of the money as to where you plan to allocate it. The "**Existing Investors**" section you **may** or **may not** wish to use it. You may not feel comfortable letting other people know who already committed money. The reason for this is that if your executive summary gets into the wrong hands, they can then approach your investor(s) and attempt to **name drop** saying that they know you and they too are looking for money. In this particular executive summary, I was honest and I simply said that the process has begun meaning I don't have any investors as of yet. You

may wish to say under the Existing Investor section "**to be supplied**" so you don't give that up unless you feel that you have a serious investor and you are past the informal aspect of dealing with a particular group.

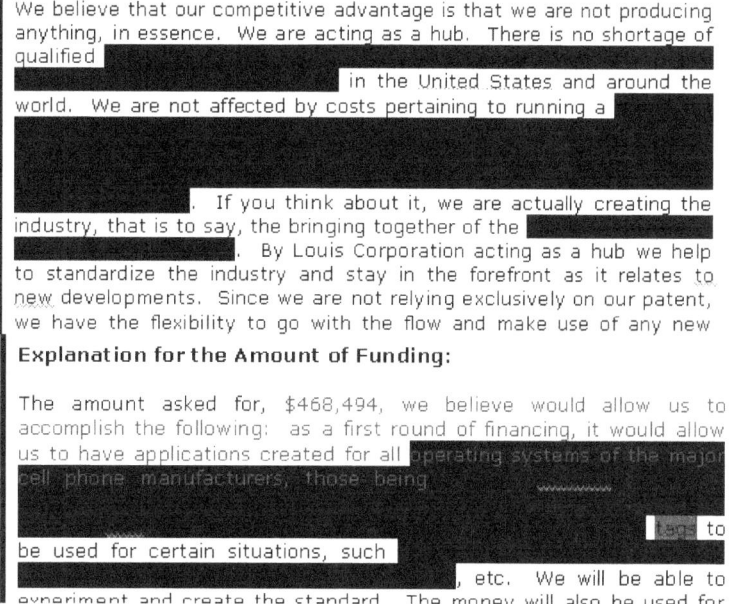

Competition:

Of course we will have competition, but we believe that with our business model it will not be hard to come by customers, since we are giving business to those who fill orders for us. Just as the world of ███████ cannot be owned by one entity, this new medium will also be too big to control exclusively, but we know that we will be able to control a fair share and should be able to have a significant share in the United States and countries around the world. Our brand recognition will help to keep our customer base climbing in an upward trend. As

Competitive Advantage:

We believe that our competitive advantage is that we are not producing anything, in essence. We are acting as a hub. There is no shortage of qualified ████████████████████████████████████ in the United States and around the world. We are not affected by costs pertaining to running a ██. If you think about it, we are actually creating the industry, that is to say, the bringing together of the ███████████████████████████. By Louis Corporation acting as a hub we help to standardize the industry and stay in the forefront as it relates to new developments. Since we are not relying exclusively on our patent, we have the flexibility to go with the flow and make use of any new

Explanation for the Amount of Funding:

The amount asked for, $468,494, we believe would allow us to accomplish the following: as a first round of financing, it would allow us to have applications created for all operating systems of the major cell phone manufacturers, those being ███ to be used for certain situations, such ██████████████████████████████████, etc. We will be able to experiment and create the standard. The money will also be used for

4.   Above, we have the "**Competition**" section and you should give a short but concise overview. Remember, you will expand heavily in your business plan so do a nice and concise job in the executive summary. The same thing for your "**Competitive Advantage**" section. Give a taste of what will place you in a great position to compete with the current companies that are already participating in the proposed line of business. Finally, in your "**Explanation for the Amount of Funding**" section if you should so choose to use it (**you may wish to just go with the info you already have in your left side panel**) just give a concise synopsis with a bit more info than shown in the left side panel.

Business Model:

The Louis business model is based off of affiliate relationships, whereby Louis Corporation does not have to ███████████████████████████████ ███████████████████████████████████ ███████████████████████████████████ ███████████████████████████████████ ███████████████████████████. We will also be part of affiliate programs where website owners who are in the three lines of business that we will be dealing with will be able to place our banners on their site, which will exponentially expose our business all over the world. ███████████████████████████████████ ██████" ████████████████████████████

Distribution/Sales Model:

Our customers will be serviced by proven companies that are already up and running and profitable for some time. █████████████████ ████████████████ will not have to re-tool in any significant fashion. Everything that will be sold on the Louis site will be produced and sent

5. For the "**Business Model**" section, attempt to do a quick summary concerning the type of business model you will be attempting to employ. Are you local and global, are you internet based, do you actually manufacture or are you totally affiliate related etc. For the "**Distribution/Sales Model**" section do a concise paragraph on how your will get your product or service into the hands of your would-be customer.

Technologies/IP:

We have Trademark Protection and have been awarded our Patent.

6. Finally, under the "**Technologies/IP**" section let the investor know what you have done, are doing or plan to do in terms of protecting the name of the product or service, the patents that have or will issue if you have a device or new disruptive business model etc. The intellectual property is important to a would-be investor because it gives value to the project. By things being protected by Trademark or Patent it simply means that you will own those items and other entities have to approach you for the legal use of those items. The items that are protected add overall value to the company and have **brand recognition** and **licensing value** as well.

Those who are Dealing with a Patent Device

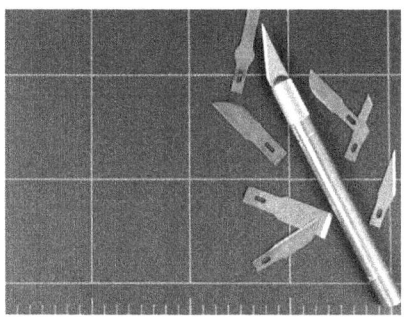

Again, I don't want to give you a book on how to get ready for a patent. If you go to lowcostempire.com, I have authored a book **Low Cost Empire Volume II, A Game Plan For Inventors**. That book gives you a strategy that you can follow which is thorough. I will, in the spirit of moving forward, give you a nice overview of what you can do concerning your patent before you go looking for money or before you let the public in on your new invention. Look, you are looking for money for one of the 3 usual things. Either you have a new concept such as a utility patent concept, a new business model or a service model or new device and you need some help getting it off the ground. The patent people (if you are one of them), not only have the patent aspect to deal with but they also have the marketing end, the production end and the intellectual property end in terms of a trademark etc. so it is much more than a guy with a napkin and a drawing. Today, in order to see real profit, you have to be organized and you have to take steps to protect and preserve your rights over the ownership of the concept or product. So, even if you are not doing a patent, I suggest you still read this chapter since you will learn a lot regardless. So, here it goes.

I want you to learn the 1) **Chronology** of a **Utility Patent Filing**. 2) I want you to learn the basic checklist of how to check if **your proposed name of your invention is available** for ownership in the form of a **Trademark**. There is no reason why you should not simultaneously be pursuing a Trademark for your patent if you have a really good concept name. 3) Finally, I want you to learn about the world of **licensing**. All of this learning I want you to do over a period of 6 months to a year depending on how quickly you learn. The books that I will recommend are inexpensive but will quickly give you a **VERY CLEAR** understanding of the Patent process and the Licensing Process. You would rather pay a **few dollars** to have invaluable knowledge than to just hand your invention over to others and say do everything for me. You need to be in charge. You also need to be able to convey to others that you are in charge and there is no doubt about it. Otherwise, you set yourself up to be taken for a lot of money and you will just end up being frustrated. So, if you think you truly have a good idea then you owe it to yourself and your family to really learn as much as you can so you can fully take part in the process and feel comfortable when doing so.

Patenting can be expensive but sometimes it is necessary. So, before you get involved with this more complicated process, I would recommend the following. For one, go to **www.uspto.gov** or if you are not in the United States you can go to the Patent and Trademark database of your country and read everything you can on the patent process. Live there for about a week. Use the search feature in the Patent data base and start to probe and search for those inventions that are **already patented** or **in the process of being patented** in the same or similar subject area of your invention.

Use key search words that you feel would turn up your invention if it were to be already out there. The key words that you use will also help to bring up patents that are in the same ball park as your invention but maybe not exactly like your invention. **You want to know what is going on in the outside world. Search for your invention to the best of your ability. You want to see whether it is out there in any way, shape or form. Maybe certain aspects of your invention are out there but not the core of your invention**. Do your best but probe probe probe. At some point down the line you will have a Patent Search performed by a Patent Attorney but you are not there yet so do the work. By you doing the preliminary work, you are also learning the pieces of a patent and all of this will be invaluable to you!

Go to **Amazon.com** and purchase the book **Patent It Yourself** by **David Pressman**. You can get this book used on either Amazon or Half.com. I have had the pleasure of corresponding with Mr. Pressman and he is the real deal and a nice guy. I have filed **two Patents** using the Pressman book. The Pressman book is going to breakdown the **chronology of filing a patent from the beginning to the end**. It is an **outstanding** book for any beginner inventor. This book alone will give you the ability to talk the talk with confidence. Go to **Inventorsdigest.com** where you will find all types of help. They are one of the best sources for **honest help** for new inventors. You will find mold makers, prototype people, electronic prototype people, graphic design people and other related services. I would recommend that you initially file a **Provisional Patent**. For a "Small Business Entity" which you are most likely to be, your cost will be $125.00 if you do it yourself. Add a few hundred dollars more if someone else does it for you.

A **Provisional Patent** will hold your conception date and **will give you up to a year to convert it over to a regular patent application**. Go to the USPTO.gov website and in the patent section look up the Provisional Patent Application. There are books on Amazon devoted to helping you file a Provisional application. The USPTO also has their own set of instructions. The Pressman book also has a lot of info on the Provisional. The Pressman book will fill you in on what you need to know in order to file a Provisional Patent as well as the USPTO.gov site. The Pressman book will also provide you with a very clear understanding of the entire Patent Application Process and how each section is drafted and how it should look. This book is very friendly in terms of the writing style and takes what could be intimidating subject matter and makes it very easy to digest and understand. **If you are an inventor, then the Pressman book is your best friend**. You are going to use the Pressman book to learn the Chronology of the Patent Process, how each individual piece is drafted and how each piece of the patent application pertains to your invention.

You may be excited about your new idea but be careful what you say. Telling others about your idea without the proper protection leaves you without any recourse if someone decides to tell others about your idea. Keep it under wraps for as long as possible. Learn as much as you can and do as much as you can by yourself. You should use **the need to know basis concept** when dealing with people. Use **Non-Disclosure/Non Compete Agreements** whenever you can. If possible, you want to get people (such as mold makers, prototypers etc.) to sign-off with a Non Disclosure at the very least that they will not divulge unnecessarily your information regarding your concept to others while you are in the process of seeking protection for your invention by having a patent granted. Control the flow of information and be careful what you divulge. You will know how much to say in each individual situation. You can talk in generality unless of course you are working with a known friend or your attorney. **Don't ever send your concept to anyone by mail or email** unless it is your attorney. Sending the invention out to someone you do not know is like handing them your concept. How can you possibly track who they show it to? Those invention companies that put in a supposed non-disclosure form and tell you to tell them your idea are in my mind bordering on criminal.

They very well know that once you take the Genie out of the bottle that you are going to lose the ability to ever capitalize on the concept. What is even worse is the fact that no matter what you send, they will tell you it is amazing and hit you with a bill in order for them to do some water downed patent. STAY AWAY FROM THEM. When you are actually ready to do a real utility patent, you will go to a patent attorney and I can give you a great recommendation. In the meantime, file a provisional patent and that will buy you time in order to learn the necessary lingo and chronology so that you can properly take part in a very important part of your professional life.

I would suggest you go to **Google** or **Startpage.com** and start searching for **Non-Disclosure/Non-Compete Agreements**. If fact, I will give you a nice Non-Disclosure/Non-Compete with complete narrative after this chapter so hold tight. When you find one that you like, tailor it to your situation. Make it very clear that you are coming to Joe Smith for prototyping services relating to my project in the field of _____. Don't be so general that the guy will not sign it since he works on technical things all the time. You want to get into his/her head that this is "**my project**" and don't even think about doing something that you will regret. Sometimes they will already have their own Non-disclosure documents but you should read them thoroughly before signing.

If a prospective person who is going to do work for you takes the attitude that they will not sign your NDA then tell them FORGET IT. What they are telling you is that they don't intend to be silenced. If they like something they see in terms of your idea or invention they will talk about to others with no repercussion. You don't need that type of individual and until you find the person who respects your intellectual property you don't let people see your stuff without them having first signed off. You need recourse. When you do find someone who signs your NDA I would recommend that you send your emails out with the Outlook email function that allows you to see when they opened it so that you are never in a position where they tell you they did not get your email. If you don't have Microsoft Outlook, look for Groupwise or go to getnotify.com in order to have the ability to know when the recipient opened it. With getnotify.com, **the recipient does not know they are being tracked**. Another thing to look for is that people will fill out all their info on the NDA but will not sign which is an old trick but one that renders the NDA useless. People play games, so things like knowing the intended recipient got your materials and opened them up stops some of the games. After all, if you are sending sensitive info to someone, you don't need them telling you that they never got it meanwhile they got it alright and they are up to no good.

Join **LinkedIn.com** and look for groups that deal with your same subject matter. You are allowed to join up to **fifty** groups for free. Being involved with these groups will allow you to see what they are talking about concerning new technology etc. and you can make valuable connections in terms of manufacturers, financial people, marketers etc. If your idea is already out there then through your groups you will have a chance to see to what extent it is, by keeping a watch on your groups and their discussions and offerings. Pick your groups one by one. If you join a group and it is off the mark and not really what you need then simply leave that group and join another that might be closer to the subject matter of your invention.

If you wish to search the internet when working on your invention then go to startpage.com. This site allows you to search without anyone else keeping track of what you are searching. If you feel you are breaking new ground then you want to operate in as stealth of a manner as possible. This site will allow you to do so without losing any searching capability. It essentially is a mask on top of Google.

(Industry/Trend Watching)

Whatever industry your business or invention falls under, you want to keep abreast of where the industry is heading, the new developments concerning inventions, procedure, new devices, new software, new partnerships, mergers, etc. By knowing the state of the art of your area of expertise, you will know whether you are doing something that is unique and innovative. If you truly are breaking new ground, then you may wish to try and protect it through the patent process by use of a **Utility** or **Design** Patent. Even if you are not breaking new ground, you can at least be keeping up with all of the industry changes so that you can serve your customers in a way that is right up to date.

It is not a good sign to a client or would be funding source if they call you to ask whether you do a particular procedure or subscribe to a particular service and you do not know what they are talking about. You owe it to your customers and yourself to keep on top of your industry so that nothing is a surprise and you always appear to be on top of your game. Now, in order to help you do this, let's discuss how to stay on top of the information flow concerning your industry. Go to magazine stores, go onto the internet, type in **trade magazines** – computers, trade magazine cooking, trade magazine real estate, trade magazine carpentry, trade magazines, etc. Whatever you do for a living there are trade magazines for your industry that talk about new advances in that industry. You can also look up "Trends in the _____ (your industry)" industry and see what pops up. By the way, **Tradepub.com** is my favorite trade magazine source. Whatever industry your invention falls under, you can get many free subscriptions to high end industry trade magazines. **This is a wealth of free information for you**. Below are some samples of Trade magazine and website sources. If you are about to deal with a patent concept then this is a must.

Publication/Site	Comments
internet retailer- STRATEGIES FOR MULTI-CHANNEL RETAILING Customers Marketing Fulfillment & Returns Industry Issues & Trends Strategies & Profiles Supply Chain Technology Web Site Trends	The **Internet Retailer** is a great magazine. It goes over all types of issues having to do with doing business over the internet, the trends, advancements, dealing with customers, strategy and services that help you fulfill orders. It also highlights certain websites and goes over them in detail for plus and minus points. Anyone that conducts business over the internet should subscribe. It is a free subscription. **http://www.internetretailer.com/**
IR NEWSLINK ＹBlueHornet THE NEWS SERVICE FOR SUBSCRIBERS OF INTERNET RETAILER Jan. 31, 2006 You are receiving this e-mail as part of your request subscription to IRNewsLink. Internet Retailer's opt-in e-mail news service, which includes four newsletter editions per week and periodic product bulletins of interest to those in the internet retailing industry. To insure delivery, please add internetretailer@verticalwebmedia.com to your e-mail address book	**IRNEWSLINK** is the e-mail news service for people who also subscribe to the Internet Retailer. In this e-mail publication you find articles on everything to do with companies doing business on-line, how people around the country and the world use the internet, what mergers are taking place and on and on. E-mail them and ask to be placed on their mailing list. Go To **internetretailer@verticalwebmedia.com**
TradePub.com A Division of NetLine Corporation	Look for your industry and this site will come up with multiple selections of magazines and white papers for you to look at concerning the effort to keep current within your industry.

 Free Subscription – Electronic and Paper	As they say on their masthead of their site: Offering in-depth analysis, perspectives, and insights on the wireless markets. www.wirelessweek.com
	Free Newsletter. Communications, consumer electronics, up and coming markets, up and coming countries. Very thorough. www.electronic.news.com
Franchise GATOR.com Connecting Entrepreneurs with Franchise and Business Opport	Franchise Gator is a top franchise and small business resource. Search franchises, opportunities and franchise business for sale listings to finding in-depth information on buying franchises and businesses for sale. **www.franchisegator.com**
PREPARED FOODS DEVELOPMENT TRENDS & TECHNOLOGIES FOR FORMULATORS & MARKETERS	People in the prepared Foods Industry: Market research, industry links, news, magazines strategies. This site is a must for anyone in the prepared foods industry. **www.preparedfoods.com**

- ▶ BRAND PACKAGING
- ▶ CANDY INDUSTRY
- ▶ CONFECTIONER
- ▶ DAIRY FIELD
- ▶ FLEXIBLE PACKAGING
- ▶ FOOD & DRUG PACKAGING
- ▶ INDUSTRIA ALIMENTICIA
- ▶ MEAT & DELI RETAILER
- ▶ THE NATIONAL PROVISIONER
- ▶ PL BUYER
- ▶ REFRIGERATED & FROZEN FOODS
- ▶ REFRIGERATED & FROZEN FOODS RETAILER
- ▶ SNACK FOOD & WHOLESALE BAKERY

Everything to do with packaging in the food industry, trends, advancements, what sells, articles, studies, great site. Go to **http://www.fdp.com/**

Market Research on Companies in the Financial Services Industry Insurance Industry

Research and trends in banking, accounting and the insurance industry

www.firstresearch.com

This quote was taken from the Trend Watching home page and it really summarizes what their site is all about.

trendwatching.com and its 8,000+ trend spotters scan the globe for emerging consumer trends.

We report on our findings in free, opinionated Trend Briefings, turning our observations into trends like INSPERIENCES, TWINSUMER, and GENERATION C.

Our subscribers in 120+ countries use our trends to dream up new goods, services and experiences for (or with) their customers.

www.trendwatching.com

As an inventor or business person, you may have the need to look for manufacturers in the United States. You can go to the Thomas site **http://www.thomasnet.com.** This site has been around for many years. It used to be called simply **The Thomas Register** and it was in book form in major libraries as well as on-line. It truly is a great resource for inventors and business owners who wish to do research on their own in terms of finding manufacturers who produce a specific item in the United States. They give you the address, the phone number and some statistical information about the different companies that are found in each search.

You will also find on the internet all types of suppliers and factories who can produce your product. Due your due diligence because you don't want to give someone your idea let us say in China only to have it reproduced all over the place and you are not being paid. They do not look at intellectual property in the same way we do. So, if you have a great idea, going to a foreign manufacturer without careful due diligence may result in you now having your idea also being produced in Europe and Asia and **you had no say about it nor did you make one cent of commission**! They know that you most probably are not going to China in order to make them stop (cease and desist) so don't be so fast to say okay to a foreign supplier because you save a few dollars. You also may lose total control where your invention ends up. **You have to be very comfortable with the supplier if you don't license out the invention to someone who already has a solid manufacturing team or division in place!**

Finally, if you are taking the Provisional Application approach, then you have a year to become very familiar with the world of licensing. I suggest you take the time to educate yourself. Do everything I tell you in this book. If you are not aware of everything that you should be aware of then "they" will see you coming from miles away. If you are to receive a patent down the road, you will be in a position to license the rights to other entities by way of Licensing Agreements. Whether another company pays you for the right to produce the item and put their own brand name on it, or to simply be a licensed dealer you need to be comfortable with the basics of licensing agreements and I **HIGHLY** recommend the book **License Your Invention** by Attorney **Richard Stim**. You can get the book at Amazon.com (plenty of used ones as well). It is a wonderful book and you will certainly be in a position to talk the talk after the book is finished. **David Pressman for the Patent Book and Richard Stim for the Licensing book should be applauded because they go over things that an attorney normally will never go over with you in this easy to understand manner but through in detail. Guess what? Pressman and Stim are best friends**.

You will get a great education from those two books. If you are a person who likes to learn then you will love those books. The idea is to educate yourself and have a game plan so that you **are not led by the nose** when you make your attempt to get a patent and market it. This education that you need to undertake is going to make it more of a possibility that you will be a success. You will be able to understand and take part in the entire process.

License Magazine is a must for people who wish to learn the licensing business. Go to their website and sign up for your free subscription. They can be found at http://www.licensemag.com.

......*

Non Disclosure – Non Compete - (NDNC)

Vocabulary For This Chapter:

NDNC – Circumvent – Irrevocably Agree--Confidentiality – Indemnification -

This is a very common contract. With the NDNC, you have a situation where **you need their service** and **they need your business**. In the case of an invention, the other side needs your business and agrees not to divulge the nature of your invention to others without your permission. So, in order to help prevent the spread of information concerning the details of your invention you enter into a Non-Disclosure Non Compete Agreement. Once both sides have entered into the Non-Disclosure Non Compete Agreement, you hope that the other side adheres to it and does not enter into agreements behind your back as soon as you reveal the thorough nature of your invention. Unfortunately, it is one of those things where unless someone somewhere is willing to take a chance to move things forward nothing will ever happen. Once you have the NDNC signed by both parties you are then in position to show your side (lawyer, would be funding person, partners) that you have entered into such agreement and it should be honored by the Inventor and the prototype person, patent drawing person or other contractor.

The object is to keep yourself in the mix where your presence and your connection to your invention is never in doubt. I will go over some of the pieces of the NDNA but right off the bat, I would suggest that when you start to read any contract, you have either a Hard Copy version of **Black's Law Dictionary** or go to thelawdictionary.org which is the Black's Law Dictionary on-line. Also, you should know that if you go to **half.com** and put in "**Black's Law Dictionary**", you will see used copies in great condition for a few dollars.

Some Essential Pieces of the NDNA Agreement

The intending parties hereby legally, and irrevocably bind themselves into guarantee to each other that they shall not directly or indirectly interfere with, circumvent or attempt to circumvent, avoid, by-pass or obviate each others interest or the interest or relationship between **"The Parties"** with procedures, seller, buyers, brokers, dealers, distributors, refiners, shippers, financial instructions, technology owners or manufacturers, to change, increase or avoid directly or indirectly payments of established or to be established fees, commissions, or continuance of pre-established relationship or intervene in un-contracted relationships with manufacturers or technology owners with intermediaries entrepreneurs, legal council or initiate buy/sell relationship or transactional relationship that by-passes one of **"The Parties"** to one another in connection with any ongoing and future transaction or project.

1. TERMS AND CONDITIONS

A. The parties to this agreement will not in any manner, directly or indirectly, solicit, nor accept any business in any manner from, nor give or provide any business in an manner to sources, contacts or the Affiliates thereof which were made available through by any other parties to this Agreement, without **express prior written permission** of the party or parties who made available the applicable sources, contacts or the Affiliates thereof.

B. The parties to this Agreement **will maintain complete confidentiality** regarding the **sources, contacts and/or the Affiliates thereof**, and will disclose such sources, contacts or the Affiliates thereof only to the named parties to this Agreement and only **pursuant to the express prior written permission of the party or parties who made available the applicable sources**, contacts or the Affiliates.

C. The parties to this Agreement will not disclose the names, addresses E-mail address, telephone and tele-fax or telex numbers of any sources, contacts or the Affiliates thereof of any party to this Agreement to third parties without the express prior written permission of the party or parties who made available the applicable sources, contacts or the Affiliates thereof , they **recognize such sources, contacts and the Affiliates thereof as the exclusive property of the respective parties to this Agreement** who made available the applicable sources, contacts or the Affiliates thereof, and they **will not enter into any direct or indirect negotiations or transactions with such sources, contacts or the Affiliates thereof** made available by or through the other parties to this Agreement

D. The parties to this agreement will not, directly or indirectly enter into or engage in any business transaction **with any banks, investors, sources of funds or other persons or entities, the names of which have been provided by one of the other parties to this Agreement**, unless the express prior written permission to permit same has been obtained from the other party (ies) providing such names. The parties to this Agreement also undertake not to make use **of any third party to circumvent** any provisions or obligations under or in connection with this Agreement.

1.   So, for starters take a careful look at the material that you see above. If your NDNC agreement does not have at least these A-D provisions, then have them added.

2.   These four paragraphs above (A-D) basically are saying that they are going to respect the fact that the concepts in your proposed patent idea are your concepts and that they will make no attempt to prosper from the information you are sharing. They will also make no move to involve a third party that will attempt to make use of the "**information**" to the detriment or exclusion of the party that originally brought forward the idea being **YOU**. The other side can say that you are going to be their client and there is absolutely nothing to worry about. This is a common statement made by contractors who work on intellectual property related ideas. Good, if there is nothing to worry about have them sign the **NDNC PERIOD!**

3.   The idea is that there are a lot of people that are always testing you to see just how aggressive you are in terms of protecting your concepts. Note that in the NDNC, if one side wishes to engage contacts from the other side that it has to be a situation where "**Express prior written permission**" **has been granted by the other side. The written permission can be done by email if it states in the contract that email is an accepted method of obtaining permission.** In this way, everyone knows what is going on at all times. So, for example, if your prototype guy comes across someone who he feels would be a perfect fit in terms of your invention, he has to talk to you about it first before he ever talks to the other person. When people start taking liberties and leaving you out of the loop, you have a major problem. If you have the type of relationship that is working, then you have a very good chance of having success since each side is respecting the other and does not want to circumvent. They just want to get things done. Let's keep going.

AGREEMENT NOT TO DISCLOSE

"**The Parties**" irrevocably agree that they shall not disclose or otherwise reveal directly or indirectly to a third party any confidential information provided by one party to the other or otherwise acquired,
particularly contract terms, product information or manufacturing processes, prices, fees, financial agreement, schedules and information concerning the identity of the sellers, producers, buyers, lenders, borrowers, brokers, distributors, refiners, manufacturers, technology

$\mathscr{Le}$	$\mathscr{Cb}$	$\mathcal{K7}$	⁴ᵗʰ Initials	5ᵗʰ Initials

NCND & Master Fee's Protection Agreements
Page 1 of 5

---

4.   Take a look at the picture directly above. Note that at the bottom of the page (the initials), each individual taking part in the NDNC is placing their initials on **each and every page bottom** to show that they have read each page **and have agreed** to the verbiage of each page. This prevents people from

signing an NDNC and saying that they never read this or they never read that in the contract.

5.   A paragraph on indemnity is important. Indemnification means that if for some reason there are monetary losses, damages, liabilities that arise relating to your dealings outside of the dealings with the signer of the NDNC that you hold the signer harmless and he does not become involved simply from association with you and because he is working on your invention.

A good example of this would be maybe you have a dispute with someone who says that they are the first person with that idea and decide to sue you and everything attached to you as per the invention that you don't drag the other person into it who was doing nothing more than doing work on your behalf. It works both ways. Maybe the person you hired is building something of yours and a fire occurs and because it was your invention he was working on he attempts to blame you for a flaw in the design and therefore sues you. The Indemnification clause would prevent him from going after you because of a mishap of some sort which resulted in monetary loss to him. So, hold each other harmless. Below is a sample of this type of paragraph:

Indemnifications; Standard of Care: ***Separate and aside from the non-disclosure non compete aspect of this NDNC agreement***, Smith and Jones agree to indemnify and hold harmless Inventor Louis Ellman and his affiliates and his respective past, present and future directors, officers, shareholders employees, and agents (the "Indemnified Parties") to the fullest lawful extent from and against any and all losses, claims, damages or liabilities (or actions in respect thereof), arising out of or related to this Agreement, any actions taken or omitted to be taken (including acts or omissions constituting ordinary negligence) in connection with the NDNC, or any transaction or proposed relationship contemplated by the NDNC; provided, however, that Smith and Jones are provided the same protections and indemnification from Inventor Louis Ellman.

6.   So in each NDNC there should be a section on **indemnity**. You will see indemnity sections in Finders Agreements, Fee Agreements and other agreements. The point is that things happen and both sides do not want to unnecessarily be dragged into something they essentially had nothing to do with other than they know the other party.

In specific deals where one of *"The Parties"* acting as an agent allows the buyers or buyer's mandate, and the seller to deal directly with one another, the agent shall be informed of the development of the transactions by receiving copies of the correspondence made between the buyer or buyer's mandate and the seller.

This agreement shall be valid for two (2) years commending from the date of this agreement. This agreement has an option to renew for a further period of five (5) years subject to and upon the terms and conditions agreed between both parties.
This agreement shall apply to:
- All transactions originated during the term of this agreement.
- All subsequent transactions that are follow up, repeat, extended or renegotiated transactions of transactions originated during the term of this agreement.

7.   Take a look above at "Agreement To Inform." Above, it is saying that each side who took part in this NDNC **will be kept informed** by receiving copies of correspondence between the Inventor and Contractor either by fax or email or regular mail.   This is very important because **if you are not getting correspondence** how will you know if something is going on or someone is talking to someone about your concept? It could have happened a month ago and they simply keep telling you that **they have not spoken to anyone. Meanwhile your concept could have been compromised a month ago and who knows how many people have now been exposed to what you intended to keep under wraps.** Anything pertaining to your project you need to be kept in the loop verbally, by email, by regular mail, by fax etc. Nothing should be going on that you are not being copied on and giving the okay to.

8.   Take a look at "**Term**" above. Two years for this type of contract to be in full effect is standard. Any longer than two years can be challenged. If the term were to be too short, then it would be very tempting for one side or the other to just lay low then as soon as the **NDNC expires**, they would immediately open their mouth or take action concerning your concept. Two years is plenty of time for you to file a Provisional or Utility patent.

Each representative signs below guarantees that he/she is dully empowered by his/her respectively named company to enter into and be bound by the commitments and obligations contained herein as individual, corporate body or on behalf of a corporate body.

1) Initial Details: 1st Party

Signatory's Full Name:	Louis Ellman
Company Name:	AdvanceTo Corporation
Position in Company:	Vice President
Address:	221-55 66th Avenue, Hempstead, NY 11385
Phone:	888-888-8888
Fax:	888-999-6666
Mobile:	347-999-9999
E-mail:	louis@advanceto.com
Skype ID:	work44
Passport/ID Number:	12345678 (L. Ellman)
Nationality:	American Citizen

Company Seal & Signature:
Signed Date: March 11, 2011

2) Initial Details: 2nd Party

Signatory's Full Name:	Stan Thurmus
Company Name:	Thurmus Consulting
Position in Company:	Principal
Address:	888 E. 86th St., New York, NY 10019
Mobile:	(212) 493-2340
E-mail:	S.Thurnus@yahoo.com
Passport/ID Number:	Available Upon Request
Nationality:	USA

Company Seal & Signatures:
Signed Date: March 11, 2011

9.   Finally, above is the signature page. Notice a very important piece of the puzzle is missing. **Can you guess what it is?** I intentionally took out the signatures for the protection of the individuals. But, you should know that if you receive an NDNC or straight up NDA (Non Disclosure Agreement) without a signature, but all of the other info is in there -- it is still worthless! I cannot tell you how many times I have received NDNC's from people that just got off the phone with a friendly demeanor and a lot of kind words only to leave out their little signature. Why did they do that? Well, think about it. If they think you are either inexperienced or just stupid, they feel you will just send them back your signature on the NDNC and then **they start to act like the NDNC is legal and in force may try to take liberties with the excuse** "what is your problem, we both have entered into the NDNC". Once the cat is out of the bag, once you cough up your hard earned information, there is no putting the information back in. They will have just successfully grabbed your concept info and you can now **kiss your idea goodbye** unless of course you have **a very good relationship** with this person and you know they would never do anything to bypass you or take your concept. Make sure any contract you receive has been signed with the proper information as to their place of business etc. In fact, before you send back your signature you do the proper due diligence and make sure that every bit of information that is placed on the NDNC checks out.

10.   Very important tip!! Request that people sign the actual NDNC and then scan the document in and make it a PDF file that they can **fax or email** to you. Too many electronic signatures take the form of a **JPG** or **GIF** and can easily have been **copied and pasted** from one document to another and therefore **the other side can contest the signature** and claim that the current agreement is invalid and still they have grabbed your invention concept. If they physically sign the piece of paper and then convert it to a PDF or fax **they can no longer claim that the signature was not placed on the document by them**. Again, unfortunately, these are some of the dirty tricks that will leave you without your invention intact. Demand they sign it or place a provision in the contract right before the signature that states that *ANYTHING THEY SEND YOU WITH A SIGNATURE WILL BE DEEMED AUTHENTIC AND ENFORCEABLE*. Too many people try to back out of things that have their signature just to gain information. It truly is weasel city and it is part of the game.

11.   The trick is to be alert to all of these tricks. Having them physically sign and send to you by fax or PDF cuts down on the attempts to **disassociate themselves** from the document. If they email it to you, you will have their **email**, **date stamp**, **time stamp** and **internet protocol information**. If they scan the hard copy, most likely they will fax it to you **from their home or office** and the fax will show the phone number it came from. What are they going to claim that a burglar came in took the document and then faxed it to you?

12   **NDNC's** are very important and I want you to focus on this chapter before you ever sign one. I have tried to give you as much insight as I could without overdoing it but I do believe that you will now know when you have a good NDNC agreement. Look for the pieces I spoke of. Just keep in mind that it is a good first step of good faith. That does not mean that you still do not have to be very guarded in how you deal with a new contact. You have to get to know the people to the best of your ability so that you know genuine interest in what you have to offer vs. interest in obtaining your concept and then disappearing which happens very often and every single day in the invention industry.

Licensing Agreements

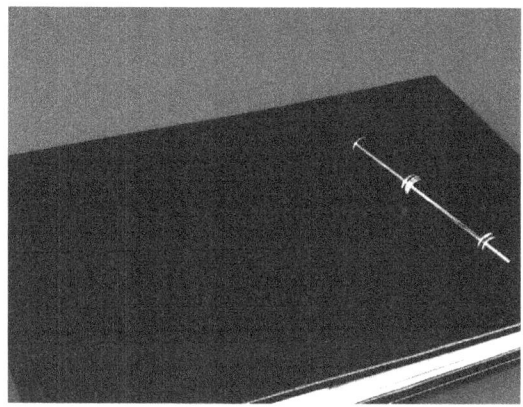

Vocabulary For This Chapter:

License Agreement—Licensor—Licensee—Trademark—Trade Secret—Royalties—Dispute Resolution—Gross Sales—Net Sales—Per Unit—Per Use—Lump Sum—Fluctuating Royalty—Hybrid License—Minimal Annual Royalty

When it comes to contracts, this particular type of agreement is very important to someone who has a patent, a trademark, a trade secret, concept that may not be patented, but nevertheless some company would like to have the ability to make use of your idea for a particular period of time. For contract issues and the entire scope of dealing with Licensing Agreements, I recommend the wonderful book entitled License Your Invention by Attorney Richard Stim. Any book that he does on the licensing of your invention or concept or service etc. is a great read and you should get a copy. Even if you are to go to **Amazon** or **Half.com** and look for a used Copy it will be well worth it since he goes over way more than the just the actual licensing agreement. We are going to go over many concepts of the Licensing type Agreement but keep in mind that Attorney Stim has authored a wonderful and thorough book for beginners-intermediate, the entrepreneur, the businessman and the layman with total focus on nothing other than licensing.

The basic components of the licensing agreement for you to think about:

Identification of the parties. The **licensor** (one who offers the opportunity) and the **licensee** (the entity that will make use of the property of the licensor).

A thorough description of the invention including patent no. What is the utility of the invention? Is there copyright material involved or is a trademark or trade secret involved as well?

If only a trademark is involved then what items will you allow a company to use your trademark on. Will there be a provision in the license that states that the potential licensee will have to identify upfront what they plan to place your trademark on and how it will be displayed. In this way, you have a chance for a thumbs up or down.

Are you protected concerning the international classification that the prospective trademark licensee wants to use your trademark on? If not, you can remedy that by filing another trademark application under the classification that was not covered. You can purchase the book "**Low Cost Empire – Getting Down To Business – Filing Your First Trademark**" for a beginning to end approach for the beginner.

A description of the licensee's products and line of business. How is the licensee planning to make use of the licensed property?

How long the license will be in effect. Will the license be in effect for a few years, for the entire length of the patent, perpetual? Will the patent expire while the license agreement is in effect?

Is the company that wants to license in good financial condition? Are they involved in any major suit?

Will this license be exclusive or can you license it out to multiple entities non-exclusive?

What territory will it cover. Is this going to be regional, local or world wide?

What is going to be allowed? For instance, I own the patent to a particular device that I am licensing out but I also have a trademark for the device which I **may or may not** allow the licensee to use.

I own a patent that can be used in **multiple industries** but only licensing it out for a **particular** industry.

Are there any provisions whereby you are able to audit the books of the licensee in order to confirm the royalties accrued?

Is there a request from the Licensee to alter the process, patent, routine etc.? How will this alteration affect your rights as a Patent holder? How will you retain 100% control?

What will be the licensing fee be and what intervals you will get paid?

What are the provisions for dispute resolution. What state will be listed for dispute resolution if you have to go to court?

Things to think about pertaining to types of Royalty Payments

Being that I just finished going through a Purchase and Sale Agreement for a patent that did not ultimately materialize, I am going to make sure that a licensing agreement as it relates to getting paid properly is thoroughly looked at. Believe me, if the licensee feels that you are somewhat green at these agreements, they will make the attempt to shade the agreement in their favor so that they can be in a position to pay you less as it pertains to the royalties that you will earn. That being said, let us take a really good look into the subject of royalties.

Gross sales: This is the total amount of money that the licensee took in from being able to make use of your patent, your trademark, your trade secret or whatever the property is that you have licensed out.

Net sales: The net sales that the company makes is composed of the gross sales minus the deductions which can take the form of costs to ship goods to customers, the cost of having to give money back to customers in the form of returns. When it is all said and done what did the company actually make off of the licensing agreement?

Royalty: The term Royalty in this respect refers to the money that the licensor earns from a percentage of the sales that the licensee brings in and it is paid out periodically. It is possible that you may receive royalty checks once a year, twice a year or every quarter. A system of *continuous royalty payments* (think of it like a tax) is sometimes referred to as a "running royalty.") On the other hand, a "**net sales royalty**", is the most common form of receiving royalty payments as a percentage of net sales. In order to calculate the amount of royalties due to you, you multiply the royalty rate that you had worked out in the agreement against the net sales amount.

1. **Royalties Based on Net Sales** As stated above, royalties based on net sales is the most common method of licensing payments. If the invention is not is not received well by the public, there will be no royalties. Licensors prefer this system because if the invention is successful, the licensor will do very well over the life of the invention. For the most part you are better off doing a royalty payment based on net sales than a lump sum payment for invention type licensing.

2. **Per Unit Royalties** In some cases, a licensor may not want to use a **royalty system based upon net sales**. An example where this could hurt the licensor is the following: For example, you are in an industry where the price of the item can drop dramatically. Although you may sell many units, if the overall net sales should drop dramatically and you have a deal where you are getting 5% of the net sales the compensation may now be much lower than it would have been before the price drop. In this case, you would be better off putting together an agreement that is tied to unit sales. So, a payment of 3 dollars per

unit may be more profitable to you than 5% of net sales in a industry where 5 percent is a very low overall amount. 5% of the oil industry is a lot different for instance than 5% of the bobbie pin industry. If you have the ability to look into a per unit royalty agreement do it I will say that if you are locked into a net sales royalty agreement then do not give the licensee an exclusive. In this way, if you are going to make less money you can make it up by opening up the flood gates as to how many licensees you have. This may be a better arrangement and a win-win situation for the licensor and the licensee.

3. **Per Use Royalties**. This type of license arrangement is good for an invention or service that people use rather than a per item purchase type of thing. For example, you patented a method of rug cleaning where your product is used as "**part of**" the overall process. Let us say that by the company using one can of this substance can clean 20 offices then you are losing out big time. You end of getting 5% of the price of the can while they got paid 20 times for the service. In this respect, the net sales system is just not worth it. Under this scenario, the licensor should insist on an In Use Royalty. This is a royalty applied to the number of times the method is used in the providing of the service. So, if we go back to our rug cleaning guys. Yes, they bought 1 bottle but used it for 20 different offices. Well, whatever the percentage is, you need to get paid on a percentage of each of the 20 offices that were cleaned using your system that was licensed to them. Even better, if you allow them to sub-license to other cleaning companies you can make a piece on all of the sub-licensees as well. Leverage is the key.

4. **Lump Sum Payments**. Lump sum payments are a way to receive licensing income without making it too complicated but this could come at a loss of revenue to you. If you are getting a one time payment for the length of the licensing agreement if the product ends up doing very well in the market place they essentially got you out the way and now they can make 100 percent on the money coming in. If I were going to take a lump sum, then I don't think I would do a licensing agreement for any more than 2 years at a time. Another thing is if I were to engage in a lump sum payment, I would not give anyone an exclusive. With the lump sum, I need to ability to offer the license to as many entities as possible. If you have a hot product, an entity might be very quick to give you the lump sum to get you out of the way for the two years so they can make the money on the license and not have to worry about sharing the profits.

5. **Fluctuating Royalty Rate**s. This is an interesting possibility. A fluctuating royalty rate (**aka a sliding royalty**) is a rate that can change during the length of the licensing due to either sales milestones or price dips. One example would be for my widget that I have licensed out. If ABC Company who licensed my widget and pays me 4% for anything up to $300,000 dollars in sales has a great year and sells $500,000 worth of widgets where anything over $300,000 earns me 6% this is a good earning year for me. So for that year I would make 4% of $300,000 and 6% of $200,000 . Similarly, a licensee may

lobby for a decreasing royalty in the event that sales fall below a certain amount. **EXAMPLE:** Mr. Smith has a device that fixes ripped clothing. He licenses the device to a company that also makes sewing machines. The royalty rate is 5% up to $100,000 in sales, 6% for anything above $100,000. But, there is a stipulation that if sales dip below $25,000 for any given year, then the royalty drops to 3%. If the company sells $25,001 worth of widgets then my 5% commission is still intact.

6. **Hybrid License Royalties**: If you are about to license a patent and a trademark or trade secret that goes along with your patent this type of licensing agreement is known as a "**hybrid license**." The hybrid license comes into play when during the period of time that the license is in effect, something about the patent or the arrangement changes. For example, for the last five years of the license agreement the patent will have expired. Therefore the amount of royalties that you will receive for the remainder of this licensing agreement will now diminish based on the agreement. When the agreement was first signed, it was determined that you would receive 15% of the net sales as your licensing royalty. It was also determined that the patent aspect would be worth 75% of the 15% royalty fee (75% of 15 = 11.25). Once the patent expires, for the remainder of the licensing agreement, they will owe you 3.75% royalty in place of the original 15% for the use of the trademark for the remainder of the agreement. As to trade secrets, this is a very touchy subject because once the cat is out of the bag so to speak it is very hard to contain the knowledge so you have to really have an iron clad agreement that the trade secret must be kept a trade secret and that the trade secret is your property. There should be **a high penalty** for not adhering to the agreement since failure to protect the trade secret could hand your secret over to the competition.

7. **Minimum Annual Royalty:** The minimum annual royalty or **guaranteed minimum royalty** is an annual payment (based on estimated royalties to be received) and is another twist to the licensing agreement in terms of royalties. In this arrangement, the licensor will receive a certain amount, regardless of how well the product performs in any given year. Each year, you receive your minimum payment. At the end of each year, the earned royalties are totaled. The earned royalties are the actual royalties that accumulated from net sales of that year. The trick is that you have to make sure that you build in a minimum annual royalty in addition to having your net sales royalty in place. If the royalties that you earn are higher than the minimum annual royalty then you will either receive a credit payment at the end of the year for the amount above the minimum annual royalty or they use that money the following year to help pay the minimum annual royalty.

Now that we have a general overview of those things that should be considered in a licensing agreement, let us now look at the components of a basic licensing agreement leading up to the license agreement.

The Initial Contract Worksheet: Whether you wish to enter into a licensing agreement or you want to offer your product, device, service, trademark, trade secret for license you need to be aware of all of those items that will be involved so this contract worksheet will help cement the items we went over in this chapter and create a very thorough license agreement.

Contract Worksheet

Licensee

Who is the licensee? What line of business, what do they do, how are they structured?

Name of Licensee Business
Licensee Address
Licensee Business Form
(1) sole proprietorship (2) general partnership limited partnership (3) corporation limited liability company
State of incorporation
Name, position and phone number of person signing for licensee

Property Definition

What to they wish to license from you? Your patent, trademark, trade secret, copyright or is it a combination?

Patent No.
Patent Application Serial No.
Copyrightable Features
Copyright Registration No.(s)
Trade Secrets
Trademarks
Trademark Registration No.(s)

Licensed Product Definition

Are you going to limit the industry they can use your licensed product in or are you going to limit the product or number of different types of products where they may make use of the licensed item. What are you going to allow your potential licensee to do?

Industry (Have you limited the license to a particular industry?)
    Product (Have you limited the license to a particular product or products

Territory

Does this potential licensee have experience in the world market or do they show their strong points in a local setting. No reason to grant them world wide rights if they do not have the ability and contacts to sell

your product or service to overseas companies. You should reserve worldwide rights for someone who is already successfully selling worldwide.

Worldwide Countries
States

Rights Granted (check those rights granted to licensee)

If you lease rights to improvements keep in mind that you need to make sure that you still own everything even though the licensee has made improvements. Otherwise, they can take the improved concept and start using it for pure profit after the licensing agreement. If they make improvements fine but you are still 100% the owner and they still need to pay you in order to be able to use the invention, trade secret or service.

Sell make or manufacture distribute
Use revise import
Lease right to improvements derivatives (copyright)
Copy (copyright) advertise promote
other rights

Rights Reserved

All rights reserved (except those granted in license)
No rights reserved
Specific rights reserved
Have you signed any other licenses? If so, do you need to reserve specific
   rights?

Term

Have you agreed upon:

I do not believe that I would grant anyone an unlimited term. It opens up too many possibilities for people to become too comfortable and take liberties with your property. I would do licensing agreements for no more than 4 or 5 years tops and revaluate. A lot of things can change within a particular company and after the license expires you may not want to re-up with that company due to changing circumstances.

A fixed term (How long?) a term limited by patent length
Unlimited term until one party terminates an initial term with renewals (see below)
other

Renewals

If you have agreed upon an initial term with renewals:

How many renewal periods? How long is each renewal period

What triggers renewal?

Licensee must notify of intent to renew.
Licensor must notify of intent to renew.
Agreement renews automatically unless Licensee indicates it does not want to
  renew.

Net Sales Deductions
What is the licensee permitted to deduct when calculating net sales?

Quantity discounts debts & uncollectibles sales commissions
Promotion and marketing costs fees freight & shipping
Credits & returns other
Is there a cap on the total amount of the deductions? Yes No
If so, how much?

Royalty Rates

Licensed Products % Combination Products %
Accessory Products %
Per Use Royalty % or Usage Standard
Other Products % Other Products %
Do you have any sliding royalty rates?
Advances and Lump Sum Payments
Advance $ _____ Date Due _____
Lump Sum Payment(s) $ Date Due _____

Guaranteed Minimum Annual Royalty

**Do you recognize all of those things that we discussed earlier? They
all come into play.**

GMAR $ _____ Date Due _____
Does the GMAR carry forward credits? Yes No
Does the GMAR carry forward deficiencies? Yes No

Audit Rights

**This is a must. If the licensee knows that you are not going to audit
their books then they will tell you what they want to tell you concerning the
sales that come from the license of your property. Push for 2 audits a year
at the least. Give them at least 5 days notice but you have to do audits
otherwise you open yourself up to being used. Human nature dictates that
when people think they can get away with something they often take
advantage of the situation.**

No. of audits permitted per year
No. of days notice

CONCLUSION

When you are starting a new business and attempting to create a new identity that puts across a certain feeling and concept there is much to consider. Before you just plunge ahead do read this book. By reading this book not only will you get ideas but you will also hopefully prevent mistakes.

A new business comes along with a new name. Remember, unless the name is truly available and unique it is most probably already claimed by another so do the work and make sure you don't waste time on names that are already in use.

I feel that when you have that unique name you will feel it and know it. Then you can go and protect it. While you are doing so, keep it under the radar until your domain name and social media are secured using this new name. Once you settle on your concept name and business name (notice I mentioned both) you can get your business cards, set up your email, your website, your social media and you are well on your way. Make sure you open your bank account so that people will be dealing with you as an entity and not an individual.

Remember, if you need help, you can email me at louisellman@gmail.com.

Once you get going, creating your identity can happen virtually overnight so go for it.

Best of luck!!!

Louis